Binge Drinking and Alcohol Misuse Among College Students and Young Adults

About the authors

Rachel P. Winograd, MA, is a graduate student in clinical psychology at the University of Missouri-Columbia, where she studies the acute effects of alcohol intoxication on behavior and emotion. She received a National Research Service Award from the National Institute of Health to conduct her dissertation work investigating "drunk personality" and geospatial characteristics of college students' recent drinking episodes. She is part of a program development group creating an evidence-based intervention for heavy drinking college students and has experience working with a range of individuals experiencing alcohol and other substance-related problems. She is a member of the Research Society on Alcoholism and the American Psychological Association.

Kenneth J. Sher, PhD, is a Curators' Distinguished Professor of Psychological Sciences at the University of Missouri-Columbia. He has published extensively on the etiology and course of substance use disorders (particularly alcohol use disorders) in later adolescence and young adulthood, and is the principal investigator on two large longitudinal studies following student drinkers during their college years and beyond. His research is funded by the National Institute of Health, and he has received over 20 awards for his teaching, mentorship, and research activities, including the Research Society on Alcoholism's Young Investigator Award, Distinguished Researcher Award, and G. Alan Marlatt Mentoring Award, as well as the American Psychological Association's Division on Addiction's Distinguished Scientific Contributions Award.

Advances in Psychotherapy – Evidence-Based Practice

Series Editor
Danny Wedding, PhD, MPH, School of Medicine, American University of Antigua, St. Georges, Antigua

Associate Editors
Larry Beutler, PhD, Professor, Palo Alto University / Pacific Graduate School of Psychology, Palo Alto, CA
Kenneth E. Freedland, PhD, Professor of Psychiatry and Psychology, Washington University School of Medicine, St. Louis, MO
Linda C. Sobell, PhD, ABPP, Professor, Center for Psychological Studies, Nova Southeastern University, Ft. Lauderdale, FL
David A. Wolfe, PhD, RBC Chair in Children's Mental Health, Centre for Addiction and Mental Health, University of Toronto, ON

The basic objective of this series is to provide therapists with practical, evidence-based treatment guidance for the most common disorders seen in clinical practice – and to do so in a reader-friendly manner. Each book in the series is both a compact "how-to" reference on a particular disorder for use by professional clinicians in their daily work and an ideal educational resource for students as well as for practice-oriented continuing education.
The most important feature of the books is that they are practical and easy to use: All are structured similarly and all provide a compact and easy-to-follow guide to all aspects that are relevant in real-life practice. Tables, boxed clinical "pearls," marginal notes, and summary boxes assist orientation, while checklists provide tools for use in daily practice.

Binge Drinking and Alcohol Misuse Among College Students and Young Adults

Rachel P. Winograd
Department of Psychological Sciences, University of Missouri-Columbia, Missouri

Kenneth J. Sher
Department of Psychological Sciences, University of Missouri-Columbia, Missouri

Library of Congress Cataloging in Publication information for the print version of this book is available via the Library of Congress Marc Database under the Library of Congress Control Number 2014956330

Library and Archives Canada Cataloguing in Publication
Winograd, Rachel P., 1984-, author
      Binge drinking and alcohol misuse among college students and young adults / Rachel P. Winograd (Department of Psychological Sciences, University of Missouri-Columbia, Missouri), Kenneth J. Sher (Department of Psychological Sciences, University of Missouri-Columbia, Missouri).

(Advances in psychotherapy--evidence-based practice ; v. 32)
Includes bibliographical references.
Issued in print and electronic formats.
ISBN 978-0-88937-403-4 (pbk.).--ISBN 978-1-61676-403-6 (pdf).--ISBN 978-1-61334-403-3 (html)

      1. College students--Alcohol use. 2. Young adults--Alcohol use. 3. Binge drinking. 4. Binge drinking--Epidemiology. 5. Binge drinking--Treatment. I. Sher, Kenneth J., author II. Title. III. Series: Advances in psychotherapy--evidence-based practice ; v. 32

HV5135.B55 2015   362.292084'2   C2014-907716-5
                                                                                              C2014-907717-3

© 2015 by Hogrefe Publishing
http://www.hogrefe.com

PUBLISHING OFFICES
USA: Hogrefe Publishing Corporation, 38 Chauncy Street, Suite 1002, Boston, MA 02111
               Phone (866) 823-4726, Fax (617) 354-6875; E-mail customerservice@hogrefe.com
EUROPE: Hogrefe Publishing GmbH, Merkelstr. 3, 37085 Göttingen, Germany
               Phone +49 551 99950-0, Fax +49 551 99950-111; E-mail publishing@hogrefe.com

SALES & DISTRIBUTION
USA: Hogrefe Publishing, Customer Services Department,
               30 Amberwood Parkway, Ashland, OH 44805
               Phone (800) 228-3749, Fax (419) 281-6883; E-mail customerservice@hogrefe.com
UK: Hogrefe Publishing, c/o Marston Book Services Ltd., 160 Eastern Ave.,
               Milton Park, Abingdon, OX14 4SB, UK
               Phone +44 1235 465577, Fax +44 1235 465556; E-mail direct.orders@marston.co.uk
EUROPE: Hogrefe Publishing, Merkelstr. 3, 37085 Göttingen, Germany
               Phone +49 551 99950-0, Fax +49 551 99950-111; E-mail publishing@hogrefe.com

OTHER OFFICES
CANADA: Hogrefe Publishing, 660 Eglinton Ave. East, Suite 119-514, Toronto, Ontario, M4G 2K2
SWITZERLAND: Hogrefe Publishing, Länggass-Strasse 76, CH-3000 Bern 9

Hogrefe Publishing
Incorporated and registered in the Commonwealth of Massachusetts, USA, and in Göttingen, Lower Saxony, Germany

No part of this book may be reproduced, stored in a retrieval system or transmitted, in any form or by any means, electronic, mechanical, photocopying, microfilming, recording or otherwise, without written permission from the publisher.

Printed and bound in the USA

ISBN 978-0-88937-403-4 (print) • ISBN 978-1-61676-403-6 (PDF) • ISBN 978-1-61334-403-3 (EPUB)
http://doi.org/10.1027/00403-000

Table of Contents

1	**Description of Young-Adult Alcohol Misuse**	1
1.1	Terminology and Definitions	1
1.1.1	Consumption	1
1.1.2	Alcohol Problems	5
1.1.3	Alcohol Dependence and Alcohol-Related Disorders	6
1.1.4	Diagnosis	7
1.2	Epidemiology and Course	10
1.2.1	Greek Organizations and Sexual Assaults on College Campuses	13
1.3	Differential Diagnosis and Comorbidities	14
1.3.1	Comorbidities	15
1.4	Diagnostic Procedures and Documentation	20
2	**Theories and Models of Alcohol Misuse**	22
2.1	Affect Regulation	23
2.2	Behavioral Undercontrol	25
2.3	Pharmacological Vulnerability	26
3	**Assessment and Treatment Indications**	28
3.1	General Issues	28
3.1.1	Self-Report Measures	28
3.1.2	Assessment Types and Options	28
3.1.3	Alcohol-Related Consequences Measures	31
3.2	Diagnosing an Alcohol Use Disorder	33
3.3	Other Assessment Domains	35
3.4	Expectancies	35
3.5	Drinking Motives	36
3.6	Readiness to Change	37
3.7	Influential Factors for Treatment	38
3.7.1	Current and Past Mental and Physical Health Problems	38
3.7.2	Treatment History	39
3.7.3	Identifying the Appropriate Treatment	40
4	**Treatment**	41
4.1	Methods of Treatment	41
4.1.1	Evidence-Based and Empirically Supported Treatment	41
4.1.2	Overview of Existing Treatment Components	41
4.2	Mechanisms of Action and Efficacy of Individual Approaches	42
4.2.1	Intervention Approach	42
4.2.2	Intervention Content	44
4.2.3	Intervention Formats	55
4.2.4	Intervention Style	58
4.3	Specific Implementation, Variation, and Combination of Methods	65

4.3.1	Brief Alcohol Screening and Intervention for College Students	65
4.3.2	Other Intervention Avenues	68
4.4	Course of Young-Adult Alcohol Misuse	70
4.5	Emerging Treatments	71
4.6	Problems Carrying Out Treatment	72
4.6.1	Preintervention Obstacles	72
4.6.2	In-Session Obstacles	73
4.6.3	Postintervention Obstacles	73
4.7	Multicultural Issues	74
4.8	Summary	75

5 Further Reading 77

6 References 78

7 Appendix: Tools and Resources 86

1

Description of Young-Adult Alcohol Misuse

Alcohol misuse is common in North America and throughout much of the industrialized and developing world. In most Western countries, alcohol problems are especially pronounced in late adolescence and early adulthood – particularly during the college years – and represent a significant public health problem. In this book, we describe the nature of alcohol misuse, its epidemiology, its causes, and methods for treatment. Fundamental to this discussion is a consideration of the basic terminology of relevant alcohol-related concepts because there are many facets of alcohol misuse, and, despite some commonalities, not all of these facets can be viewed as interchangeable from a clinical or public health perspective.

1.1 Terminology and Definitions

We use the terms *alcohol misuse* and *alcohol problems* to refer to a range of phenotypic behaviors and conditions. These terms are used by clinicians, public health workers, and researchers to describe different types of consumptive behaviors and consequences.

1.1.1 Consumption

Perhaps the most basic concept in characterizing alcohol involvement is alcohol consumption. At a fundamental level, though people can be classified as drinkers or abstainers, the classification of drinkers represents a large and highly diverse group that includes those who drink in moderation and those whose drinking patterns put them at risk for a range of consequences. It is important to note that current diagnostic criteria for alcohol-related disorders – alcohol use disorders (AUDs), according to the *Diagnostic and Statistical Manual of Mental Disorders,* 5th Edition (DSM-5; American Psychiatric Association, 2013), and alcohol dependence and hazardous use, according to the *International Statistical Classification of Diseases and Related Health Problems,* 10th Edition (ICD-10; World Health Organization (WHO), 2008) – both described below – fail to include direct measures of alcohol consumption despite the health-relevance of excessive alcohol consumption. Although not presenting formal diagnostic criteria, the US government has published safe-drinking guidelines as part of their 2010 *Dietary Guidelines for Americans*

AUD diagnostic criteria do not include measures of consumption, such as how much or how often someone drinks

> **Healthy drinking limits according to the National Institutes of Health:**
> **Men:** No more than 14 drinks per week or four drinks per occasion
> **Women:** No more than seven drinks per week or three drinks per occasion

(US Departments of Agriculture and of Health and Human Services, 2010). Moderate consumption of alcohol is defined as ≤ 2 drinks a day for men and ≤ 1 drink a day for women. Drinking ≥ 15 drinks a week for men and ≥ 8 drinks a week for women, or ≥ 5 drinks in a given day for men or ≥ 3 drinks in a given day for women is considered *high-risk* drinking, based on epidemiological data documenting increased health-related risks that occur at those consumption levels. One study found that almost one half of men and one third of women drinkers in the United States exceed these safe-drinking levels (Dawson, Grant, & Li, 2005).

In addition, there has been increasing concern in recent years over drinking patterns associated with high levels of consumption on drinking days (i.e., *binge* drinking). The US National Institute of Alcohol Abuse and Alcoholism (NIAAA) defines binge drinking as "a pattern of drinking alcohol that brings blood alcohol concentration (BAC) to 0.08 g/dL or above. For the typical adult, this pattern corresponds to consuming 5 or more drinks (male), or 4 or more drinks (female), in about 2 hours" (NIAAA, 2011). Such patterns represent significant risk for the drinker and for society. It is important to note that the five/four binge drinking definition can be a problem, as not everyone in this 2-hr time period will exceed a 0.08 g/dL BAC. Conversely, some drinkers who drink less than the five/four binge drinking threshold might achieve a BAC greater than 0.08 g/dL. The reason for such variability is related to the wide variation among men and among women in their body masses, stomach contents at the time of drinking, individual differences in alcohol metabolism rates (pharmacokinetics), and other individual factors that can vary substantially from one person to another (e.g., Cederbaum, 2012). In addition, it is possible that a different threshold might be better for identifying individuals likely to have alcohol-related difficulties. Despite any problems with a five/four threshold definition, it represents a useful metric to convey to the public what is considered a risky level of consumption and for amassing statistics on rates of heavy alcohol consumption. Note that use of the term *binge drinking* to describe this phenomenon is controversial (see Wechsler & Nelson, 2001), with some researchers arguing against its use because the term has historically been used to denote a more extreme drinking phenomenon sometimes observed in individuals with severe alcohol dependence (i.e., a "bender," a period of continuous intoxication lasting a day or more). Consequently, sometimes in the research literature the term *heavy episodic drinking* is used to describe binge drinking, with those who binge more than once a week being classified as *frequent heavy drinkers*.

> **NIAAA definition of binge drinking:** five or more drinks (for men) or four or more drinks (for women) within a 2-hr period

Extreme Consumption and Heavy Drinking Events

Drinking patterns among heavy drinking college students and young adults tend to be highly patterned as a function of day of the week, major holidays, academic breaks, and personal milestones. Studies of daily drinking over the course of the calendar year indicate that college students often engage in weekend-like drinking during the week (e.g., "Thirsty Thursdays"; Wood, Sher, & Rutledge, 2007) and that some holidays and events are strongly associated with particularly high spikes in alcohol consumption (Neighbors et al., 2011). These include traditional holidays (e.g., New Year's Day, Fourth of July), regional holidays with strong drinking traditions, sporting events (e.g., Super

Bowl), and traditional drinking rites of passage (e.g., 21st birthday, Spring Break). Moreover, college students and young adults are known for their methods of drinking that facilitate extremely heavy consumption, such as drinking heavily before leaving for a party ("prepartying") and playing drinking games.

Day of the Week

One aspect of college-age drinking that sets it apart from the typical drinking patterns of older adults is the frequent heavy drinking that occurs on Thursday nights, in addition to the usual Friday and Saturday night drinking. Often called "Thirsty Thursday" (Wood, Sher, & Rutledge, 2007), Thursday night drinking can be just as heavy as weekend drinking, and does not have the same repercussions as Monday, Tuesday, or Wednesday night drinking, because many college campuses offer fewer classes on Fridays, essentially separating it from the typical academic week. In fact, researchers have found that students who did not take Friday classes drank twice as much as students with Friday early morning classes (Wood, Sher, & Rutledge, 2007), and a NIAAA committee has suggested that administrators consider increasing the number of Friday morning classes to curtail excessive Thursday night drinking (Malloy, Goldman, & Kington, 2002).

Twenty-First Birthday Celebrations

Perhaps epitomizing the extremes that characterize some drinking during this stage of life is the phenomenon of 21st birthday drinking, when many young adults attempt to drink "21 for 21" (i.e., a drink for each year of the person's life). Although not all young drinkers attempt to accomplish this particular drinking milestone, for almost half of those drinking to celebrate their 21st birthday, this one occasion will represent the heaviest drinking event of their life to date (Rutledge, Park, & Sher, 2008). Although many young adults intend to consume large quantities of alcohol on that occasion, on average, celebrants drink more than intended, especially if they drink quickly, drink shots, and engage in various 21st birthday rituals. Given the high levels of consumption, it is not surprising that these celebrations are associated with a range of negative acute risks from drinking, including high rates of vomiting, blackouts, hangovers, physical impairment, and engaging in sexually provocative behavior. Recently, Neighbors et al. (2011) estimated the mean blood alcohol concentration (BAC) experienced by a sample of college undergraduates in the year they turned 21 years of age, across a range of different drinking events. Twenty-first birthday celebrations led the list, with estimated BACs of 0.19 g/dL (more than twice the legal limit for driving while intoxicated). Several other events are also associated with mean BACs over 0.08 g/dL (e.g., New Year's Eve and Day, Super Bowl, Mardi Gras, St. Patrick's Day, Spring Break, Cinco de Mayo, graduation, and Fourth of July). Not surprisingly, these events have been targeted for event-specific, preventive interventions (e.g., Neighbors et al., 2012).

Spring Break

Though 21st birthday celebrations may represent the extreme of heavy drinking events, there are a number of events that have been associated with very heavy drinking during the college years, such as Spring Break for students. Spring Break drinking resembles weekend drinking, and each day of vacation is like a weekend day. In addition to considering how specific events are superimposed upon what is, for many, already a heavy drinking stage of life, there are a number of other activities that are common in early adulthood that are further associated with heavy drinking, such as involvement with drinking games and drinking prior to attending certain events which are themselves associated with further drinking (e.g., prepartying, pregaming, and preloading).

Drinking Games

Drinking games refer to a diverse range of activities that are structured as games or competitions, involve the consumption of alcohol, and are associated with extreme drinking. One recent typology (LaBrie, Ehret, & Hummer, 2013) classified 100 drinking games into five different categories: (1) *targeted and skill games* (i.e., games that have a single loser who has to drink or a winner who gets to choose who drinks), (2) *communal games* (i.e., games in which everyone participates simultaneously following an agreed-upon set of rules as to when and how much is to be consumed – such as when certain events occur in a movie or TV show), (3) *chance games* (e.g., where how much someone drinks is determined by a random process such as drawing cards or rolling dice), (4) *extreme consumption games* (e.g., games involving downing one or more standard drinks quickly, like using a "beer bong" or doing a "keg stand"), and (5) *even competition games* (e.g., various individual or team games where the losers are obligated to drink). Participation in these drinking games has been associated with heavy consumption, although, not surprisingly, extreme consumption games were associated with the highest drinking levels. Though drinking games are typically associated with collegiate life and a large proportion of college students participate in them, many students come to college already having substantial experience with these games. In fact, one study (Borsari, Bergen-Cico, & Cary, 2003) found that a majority of incoming freshmen reported involvement in drinking games in high school, and their involvement in college represented more of a continuation of this behavior than an initiation. The motivations behind drinking game involvement have been explored in a number of studies, and, as summarized by Borsari et al. (2003), drinking games provide a form of structured interaction, a quick way to get drunk and readily induce a sense of camaraderie among participants. Though there is little empirical research on drinking game involvement following college, it seems likely that as the social structure of drinking changes, the frequency of engaging in drinking games does as well, and drinking games do not appear to be as prominent a feature of drinking further into adulthood.

Pregaming, Prepartying, and Preloading

In recent years, there has been increased attention to the phenomenon referred to as pregaming, prepartying, or preloading, where people drink *prior* to going out to a drinking event (e.g., bar or party) where they continue to drink. In a recent study where the BACs of a large sample of student and nonstudent adult bar patrons in a college town were directly assessed (Barry, Stellefson, Piazza-Gardner, Chaney, & Dodd, 2013), those who had pregamed had significantly higher BACs, and pregaming explained 11% of the variation in BAC. Pregaming appears to be highly prevalent in college students. One recent multicampus study of freshmen and sophomores showed that 75% of drinkers

> Events and drinking methods commonly associated with young-adult binge drinking include Thursday night drinking, 21st birthday celebrations, Spring Breaks, Drinking Games, pregaming/ prepartying/ preloading

engaged in pregaming, and it accounted for almost one third of all drinking occasions examined (Barnett, Orchowski, Read, & Kahler, 2013). Importantly, pregaming was associated with about a two-drink difference in total consumption and a 0.04 g/dL BAC increase over non-pregaming-drinking BACs. Moreover, involvement in pregaming may be associated with drinking problems over and above that predicted by total number of drinks consumed, suggesting that some contextual variables might further increase risk.

Examining the nature of young adults' drinking can provide clinicians with useful information about ways to reduce the frequency and intensity of their clients' drinking that is either already risky or heading in the direction of being risky. It is important to note that some of the drinking events and methods highlighted in this section are associated with strong environmental goads toward drinking, something that both clinicians and clients need to understand and explore. Though the heaviest drinkers are those most likely to engage in activities that lead to binge and extreme drinking, in each of these drinking situations (e.g., Spring Break, drinking games, and pregaming), it is often those less experienced who are at greatest risk for negative consequences (e.g., Lee, Lewis, & Neighbors, 2009).

1.1.2 Alcohol Problems

Although excessive consumption can be a problem in its own right, for many years, social epidemiologists have studied the overall prevalence and distribution of individual problems that are associated with alcohol. Simply stated, alcohol problems are consequences of alcohol consumption, that are associated with harm or are undesired (see Table 1).

We can think of consequences as resulting from acute effects of alcohol (i.e., effects attributable to a discrete drinking episode) such as alcohol blackouts (i.e., total loss of memory for part of a drinking episode) or a hangover, or from chronic effects of alcohol use (e.g., alcoholic cirrhosis). Moreover, alcohol can cause problems in a number of domains including health (e.g., gastrointestinal diseases, cardiac diseases, neurological impairment, sexual dysfunction, unintentional injuries), occupation, and schooling (e.g., job loss,

Table 1
Alcohol Problems

Type of effect	Example
Acute	Blackout (memory loss), vomiting, headache/hangover
Chronic physical	Cirrhosis, gastrointestinal problems
Occupational	Academic failure, job loss
Legal	Driving while intoxicated (DWI), public intoxication, minor in possession (MIP)
Social	Physical fights, verbal arguments, relationship difficulties

academic failure), legal repercussions (e.g., arrests for driving while intoxicated, public intoxication, minor in possession), and social problems (e.g., physical fights, arguments, relationship difficulties). Though in some cases, one can be confident in attributing alcohol as a sole cause of certain consequences (e.g., memory loss or a staggering gait during an episode of heavy intoxication in an otherwise healthy person), in other cases, the attribution of alcohol as a cause of consequences (e.g., erratic driving while mildly intoxicated, getting into fights after drinking) is less clear. This is because both drinking itself and drinking to intoxication are associated with individual characteristics that could be related to the consequences. That is, individuals who are more aggressive are more likely both to drink and to display aggression when intoxicated (Giancola, 2000). Similarly, individuals who drink and drive are likely to be risky drivers when not drinking (Donovan, 1993). It thus seems reasonable to assume that the extent to which a consequence is directly related to one's drinking is variable, and, depending upon the nature of the problem, one must be careful in definitively ascribing a problem as alcohol-related. Medical epidemiologists routinely employ the concept of alcohol attributable fraction (AAF) to statistically describe the presumed proportion of variance that alcohol accounts for in various conditions and disease states (e.g., Rehm et al., 2009), in recognition of the multiple causes of most medical diseases. Similarly, many purported consequences of alcohol consumption are likely determined by multiple factors, and thus it is important to remember that there is a large contribution of the drinker as well as the drink and of the context in which drinking occurs, to the occurrence and severity of an alcohol-related consequence. This may be especially true when alcohol is used strategically in a social situation to provide an "excuse" for anticipated failure and potentially in situations where alcohol is consumed to overcome one's inhibitions (i.e., "liquid courage").

The types of problems most frequently reported by young-adult drinkers are those associated with excessive consumption such as blackouts, hangovers, throwing up, interpersonal conflicts, illegal behaviors, regretted sexual behaviors, academic or vocational impairment, and engaging in hazardous behaviors (e.g., unprotected sex, driving while intoxicated). Several alcohol problem scales described later provide inventories of these and other events that are particularly relevant for young adulthood and can be of value in assessing and developing feedback for clients. It is important to note that many young adults can endorse a litany of problems encountered from drinking but not report "having an alcohol problem," and some consequences that are seen as "problems" to clinicians or society in general might not be so viewed by younger problem drinkers. Consequently, a clinician cannot assume that a problem *experienced* is a problem *perceived*. Clinicians can use a motivational approach and the type of language described later in this book (e.g., reflect what the drinker says; have drinkers give voice to what kinds of problems their continued risky drinking might cause them) when talking with such drinkers, to avoid resistance.

1.1.3 Alcohol Dependence and Alcohol-Related Disorders

Almost 40 years ago, Griffith Edwards and Milton Gross were careful to distinguish alcohol dependence from alcohol-related consequences (or disabilities)

(Edwards & Gross, 1976). These scholars used the term alcohol-related consequences to refer to a variety of negative life events that appeared to result from the acute and/or chronic effects of alcohol consumption. This was in contrast to the concept of alcohol dependence syndrome (ADS) or alcohol dependence, in which physiological signs and symptoms of dependence were indicators but not necessary criteria for the diagnosis of dependence. More specifically, the notion of alcohol dependence referred to a syndrome comprising a variety of signs and symptoms that signified the importance that alcohol consumption has come to play in the drinker's life. These signs and symptoms included what Edwards and Gross described as "a narrowing of the drinking repertoire," centrality of drinking in the person's life relative to other life tasks and responsibilities, tolerance and withdrawal, "awareness of the compulsion to drink," and rapid reinstatement of dependence symptoms after a period of abstinence (Edwards & Gross, 1976). Both substance-related consequences and the dependence syndrome can be viewed as correlated, dimensional constructs that are graded in intensity from absent to severe and do not explicitly reference the *amount* of substance consumed as a criterion (see Edwards, 1986).

1.1.4 Diagnosis

Currently, alcohol-related disorders can be diagnosed according to two major diagnostic systems: that of the *Diagnostic and Statistical Manual of Mental Disorders*, 5th Edition (DSM-5), published by the American Psychiatric Association (2013), and that of the *International Statistical Classification of Diseases and Related Health Problems*, 10th Edition (ICD-10), published by the World Health Organization (WHO, 2008). Though the DSM has previously been relied upon by American clinicians, researchers, health insurance companies, and others to make and study psychiatric diagnosis, it is scheduled to be replaced in October of 2015 by the ICD for most clinical purposes (APA Practice Organization – Practice Central, 2014; see also in Section 3.2) Specifically, clinicians will be required to bill insurance companies using ICD code sets instead of DSM codes. Because the majority of those in psychology-related fields have been trained on earlier versions of the DSM, but will soon need to adopt the language of the ICD, we provide a brief discussion of the terminology, criteria, and issues relevant to alcohol-related disorders presented in the *Diagnostic and Statistical Manual of Mental Disorders*, 4th Edition (DSM-IV), the DSM-5, and the ICD-10 diagnostic systems in the sections that follow.

Alcohol Use Disorder in the DSM
In the DSM-IV (American Psychiatric Association, 1994), AUDs used to be represented by two diagnoses: alcohol abuse and alcohol dependence. Alcohol abuse was a residual category for a pathological pattern of drinking characterized by consequences but without evidence of physiological dependence. Specifically, it was defined as

> a maladaptive pattern of substance use leading to clinically significant impairment or distress as manifested by one (or more) of the following occurring within a 12-month period: (1) recurrent substance use resulting

in a failure to fulfill major role obligations at work, school, or home, (2) recurrent substance use in situations in which it is physically hazardous, (3) recurrent substance-related legal problems, and (4) continued substance use despite having persistent or recurrent social or interpersonal problems caused or exacerbated by the effects of the substance. (American Psychiatric Association, 1994, p. 198)

In contrast, a diagnosis of alcohol dependence was intended to be consistent with the Edwards and Gross notion of the ADS (Edwards & Gross, 1976). Specifically, it was defined as a maladaptive pattern of use, leading to clinically significant impairment or distress, as manifested by three (or more) of the following symptoms occurring at any time in the same 12-month period: (1) tolerance; (2) withdrawal; (3) the substance is often taken in larger amounts or over a longer period than intended; (4) a persistent desire or unsuccessful efforts to cut down or control substance use; (5) a great deal of time is spent in activities necessary to obtain the substance, use the substance, or recover from its effects; (6) important social, occupational, or recreational activities are given up or reduced because of substance use; and (7) the substance use is continued despite knowledge of having a persistent or recurrent physical or psychological problem that is likely to have been caused or exacerbated by the substance (American Psychiatric Association, 1994). According to the DSM-IV's diagnostic hierarchy, individuals who met criteria for alcohol dependence did not receive diagnoses for alcohol abuse, implying that dependence was the more severe of the two AUDs.

However, in the recently published DSM-5 (American Psychiatric Association, 2013), the abuse/dependence distinction is abandoned in favor of a single AUD diagnosis that includes in its criteria set symptoms of both abuse and dependence (for a total of 11 symptoms). To obtain a diagnosis, clients must endorse at least two symptoms as occurring within a 12-month period (2–3 symptoms produces a diagnosis of "mild," 4–5 of "moderate," and ≥ 6 of "severe"). In addition to the added severity specifiers, other major changes to the DSM-5 AUD diagnosis include the inclusion of craving (long considered a hallmark symptom of dependence, which was included in the ICD-10 and not included in DSM-IV) and the dropping of legal problems (a DSM-IV abuse symptom that has proven to be problematic on psychometric grounds). Although DSM-5 AUD is ostensibly more severe at threshold than DSM-IV AUD, in requiring a minimum of two symptoms (instead of one for DSM-IV abuse), there is still concern that the new criteria remain too liberal and will yield artificially high prevalence rates (Martin, Steinley, Vergés, & Sher, 2011) with most diagnosed cases manifesting low levels of pathology. In addition, critics (e.g., Martin, Sher, & Chung 2011) do not believe that one of the most prevalent symptoms of substance use disorder (SUD), hazardous use, should be included as a diagnostic criterion, since it is not clearly anchored in substance-related pathology. That is, repeated heedless use may reflect little more than incautious behavior that is simply being manifested by use of the substance but is not specific to it. Why should there be a "hazardous use" symptom of AUD when other hazardous behaviors (e.g., reckless driving or texting while driving, both particularly common in young adulthood) are not similarly pathologized? Despite these concerns on conceptual and clinical grounds, the new criteria were designed, in part, to yield prevalence rates roughly comparable to DSM-IV and, thus, may show little practical difference in epidemiology. Indeed, one recent analysis of adults aged 21 and over in the United States showed that the past-year prevalence of AUD increases from 9.7% to 10.8% when moving from using DSM-IV criteria to DSM-5 (Dawson, Goldstein, & Grant, 2013), although a large minority of individuals with DSM-IV alcohol abuse failed to be diagnosed with DSM-5 AUD, and some mildly affected individuals were diagnosed as having an AUD under DSM-5 who did not meet DSM-IV criteria; in contrast, those individuals who met criteria for DSM-IV dependence were typically diagnosed under DSM-5 AUD criteria (and tended to have endorsed four or more of the 11 symptoms). As noted by Dawson et al. (2013), the change from DSM-IV to DSM-5 may have minimal practical consequences for the clinician because those who met criteria for DSM-IV dependence are likely to endorse four or more symptoms under DSM-5. However, it can be argued that the abandonment of the concept of dependence is premature, especially since the concept of AUD no longer has a conceptual core and because many of those individuals who will be diagnosed at threshold (i.e., endorse two of 11 AUD symptoms) under DSM-5 will have minimal symptomatology. The concept of dependence remains clinically and etiologically meaningful because it connotes that the nature of the problem is internal and associated with drinking motivation related to neuroadaptation and the development of compulsive alcohol seeking. This is quite different from someone who misuses alcohol as part of a more general risk-taking and heedless lifestyle, where alcohol is often a manifestation of a broader externalizing problem.

Alcohol-Related Disorders in the ICD

The 10th edition of the *International Classification of Diseases* (ICD-10; WHO, 2008) contains two alcohol-related diagnoses that are most relevant to young-adult alcohol misuse and problems: (1) harmful use and (2) dependence syndrome (the ICD-10 also includes diagnoses of acute intoxication and withdrawal state, but these are less pertinent for clinical practice with young adults and therefore will not be discussed further here). The harmful use category is defined by "a pattern of psychoactive substance use that is causing damage to health. The damage may be physical (as in cases of hepatitis from the self-administration of injected drugs) or mental (e.g., episodes of depressive disorder secondary to heavy consumption of alcohol)" (p. 69). Though this classification sounds superficially similar to the "hazardous use" criterion in DSM-5, note that the ICD-10 harmful use diagnosis extends only to changes in health status (physical or mental) that are associated with alcohol consumption and does not cover the area of "risky" behavior, which is the primary thrust of the DSM-5 hazardous use criteria. Among the reasons to include the hazardous use diagnosis in the ICD-10 is that it is well-defined and responds to medical and/or psychological treatment, as is evidenced by an empirical basis of the disorder remitting in response to therapy (e.g., Bertholet et al., 2005). In contrast, a dependence syndrome diagnosis – considered the central alcohol-related diagnosis in the ICD-10 (WHO, 2008, p. 69) – is partially defined by "a cluster of physiological, behavioral, and cognitive phenomena in which the use of a substance or a class of substances takes on a much higher priority for a given individual than other behaviors that once had greater value," which is much like Edwards and Gross's "narrowing of the drinking repertoire" concept described earlier. Additionally, at least three of the following six symptoms need to be endorsed to meet criteria for a dependence syndrome diagnosis: (1) a strong desire or sense of compulsion to take the substance; (2) difficulties in controlling substance-taking behavior in terms of its onset, termination, or levels of use; (3) a physiological withdrawal state when substance use has ceased or been reduced, as evidenced by the characteristic withdrawal syndrome for the substance, or use of the same (or a closely related) substance with the intention of relieving or avoiding withdrawal symptoms; (4) evidence of tolerance, such that increased doses of the psychoactive substances are required to achieve effects originally produced by lower doses; (5) progressive neglect of alternative pleasures or interests because of psychoactive substance use, increased amount of time necessary to obtain or take the substance or to recover from its effects; (6) persisting with substance use despite clear evidence of overtly harmful consequences, such as harm to the liver through excessive drinking, depressive mood states consequent to periods of heavy substance use, or drug-related impairment of cognitive functioning (WHO, 2008, p. 70). Efforts should be made to determine that the user was actually, or could be expected to be, aware of the nature and extent of the harm (all ICD-10 diagnostic and criteria information is publically available at http://www.who.int/substance_abuse/terminology/ICD10ClinicalDiagnosis.pdf). Because a diagnosis of ADS is considered more severe, it supersedes the harmful use diagnosis. Though draft ICD-11 criteria (ICD-11 Beta Draft) suggest that the ICD distinction between the dependence syndrome and harmful use will remain and will not be combined as in the DSM-5, this will not be finalized until sometime in 2015 (WHO, 2014).

Diagnostic "Issues"

In terms of conceptualizing and diagnosing clinical cases, the information presented here on both the DSM-5 and the ICD-10 is immediately relevant to clinicians, as the American Psychological Association (APA) encourages clinicians to still use the DSM-5 to arrive at diagnostic conclusions, even though the ICD-10 codes will be used for billing purposes (APA Practice Organization – Practice Central, 2014). Specifically, the DSM-5 contains ICD-10 code sets next to each diagnosis, allowing clinicians to make a diagnosis according to DSM-5 criteria while still being able to use ICD-10 code sets for billing purposes without needing to switch between two different documents to do so. However, it may be useful for clinicians to note that there are only two ICD-10 codes for the three different severity levels of AUD in the DSM-5. (The code for "mild" AUD corresponds to harmful use/alcohol abuse, and the codes for "moderate" and "severe" are the same and correspond to ADS.)

1.2 Epidemiology and Course

Though ICD-10 terminology and coding sets will become increasingly used in clinical settings, the vast majority of existing and recent alcohol-related research has been conducted based on the criteria and diagnoses presented in the DSM-IV. As such, most of the material in this section discussing the causes, courses, and comorbidities of alcohol-related disorders is from research conducted on AUDs, in the language of the DSM-IV (specifically, alcohol abuse and dependence are discussed as distinct constructs even though in the current DSM-5 they are merged).

Population-based, epidemiological surveys indicate that the AUD prevalence rates are high, especially among young adults. Over the past 30 years, there have been five large-scale, population-based epidemiological surveys. These studies indicate very high past-year and lifetime prevalence rates of AUDs in the general population of US adults 18 years and older. For example, in the National Epidemiological Survey on Alcohol and Related Condition (NESARC; Grant et al., 2004), 30.3% of US adults met lifetime and 8.46% met past-year DSM-IV AUD criteria. Generally, men are more likely to be diagnosed with AUDs than women. There are clear ethnic differences in the prevalence of AUDs, with Whites, Hispanics, and Native Americans having higher rates than African Americans and Asian Americans.

The prevalence of AUDs in the United States and much of the rest of the world is strongly age-graded. Figure 1 illustrates the dramatic age gradient with peak prevalence for both abuse and dependence occurring early in the third decade of life, with large decreases in prevalence clearly evident by age 30 (see Figure 1). These prevalence rate changes for AUDs over the life course

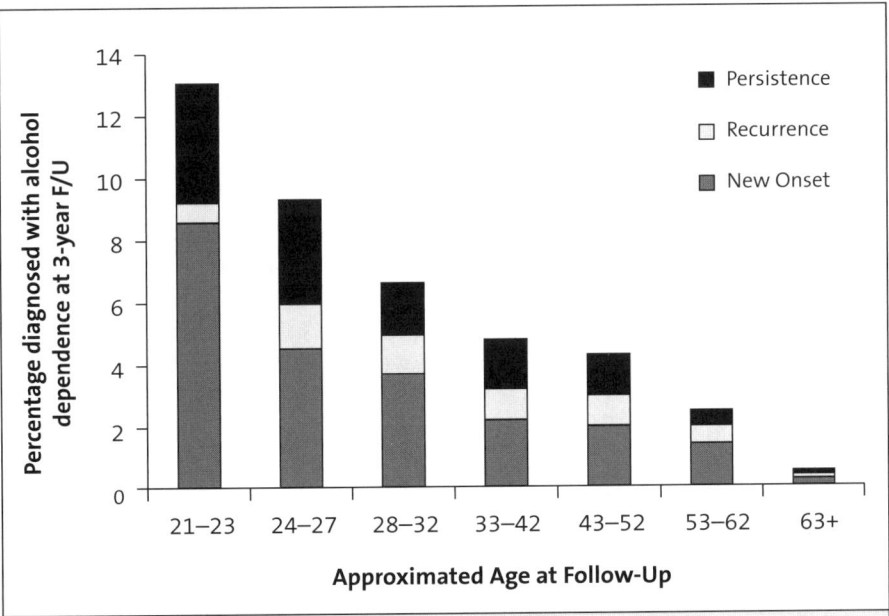

Figure 1
Relative contribution of the three alcohol dependence groups to the overall alcohol dependence prevalance across age groups. The *y*-axis represents the percentage of participants diagnosed with past 12-month alcohol dependence at Wave 2. Age groups were created on the basis of age reported at Wave 1, so that the *x*-axis shows the approxiated age at Wave 2. F/U = follow-up; *n* = total number of participants within each age group.
Adapted from Vergés et al. (2012).

> **Highest risk for AUD is between the ages of 18 and 25, a period often referred to as emerging adulthood**

suggest that we should consider AUDs, at least in part, to be a developmental disorder of young adulthood. In the United States, the period between adolescence and adulthood reflects when individuals are at the highest risk for manifesting an AUD, with the peak onset for both alcohol abuse and dependence occurring around 20 years of age. The age prevalence curve for binge drinking is similar to that for AUDs. Across four national surveys from 1993 to 2001, the highest rates of binge drinking were observed in the age strata associated with late adolescence (18–20 years of age, 19.6%–26.1%) and young adulthood (21–25 years of age, 26.5%–32.2%); these rates fall off considerably later in adulthood (26–34 years of age, 19.5%–21.3%; 35–54 years of age, 11.7%–13.6%; and > 55 years of age, 3.8%–4.3%) – see Table 2.

Table 2
Rates of Binge Drinking Across Age Groups

Age range	Percentage who binge drink
18–20	19.6%–26.1%
21–25	26.5%–32.2%
26–34	19.5%–21.3%
35–54	11.7%–13.6%
> 55	3.8%–4.3%

It is important to note that this age gradient reflects both the *prevalence* of binge drinking as well as the *intensity* of binge drinking. Similar to what occurs with AUDs, men engage in binge drinking more frequently than women, and Whites and Hispanics binge more frequently than African Americans. In addition, though the young-adult age stratum is most strongly associated with the highest rates of binge drinking, it is paradoxically associated with the lowest *perceived* risk from this type of drinking problem. Likewise, this period of life is also associated with the largest gap between "need for treatment of alcohol use" and receiving specialized services for this problem. This heightened risk for alcohol misuse and binge drinking is thought to reflect a life stage when individuals are relatively free of adult responsibilities but unrestrained by parental influence. However, as individuals progress into adulthood, and assume adult responsibilities (e.g., marriage, parenthood, jobs), rates of AUDs typically decrease, a phenomenon that is known as "maturing out" (e.g., O'Malley, 2004). Though maturing out has traditionally been attributed to the assumption of adults roles creating incompatibility between these roles and a heavy drinking lifestyle, other developmental changes occurring within the person, especially changes in personality traits associated with normative adult development, also appear to be related to a reduction in alcohol problems during the third decade of life (Littlefield, Sher, & Wood, 2009). That is, reductions in alcohol misuse reflect more than vocational and family constraints and are likely influenced by more general aspects of psychosocial maturity.

Although the age prevalence curve in Figure 1 suggests that maturing out is largely a phenomenon of young adulthood, chronicity rates for AUDs appear to be surprisingly consistent over the life course. Specifically, as noted by Vergés and colleagues:

> the notion of a "developmentally limited alcoholism" reflects not so much a different *species* of [alcohol dependence] but rather the fact that [alcohol dependence] is not highly stable at any age, but the high hazard rates of emerging adulthood give the superficial appearance that early onset alcohol disorders are less stable than those later in life. (Vergés et al., 2012, p. 518)

Notably, there is significant cultural variation in these developmental patterns. For example, African American men are likely to have later age onset of AUDs with increases during the third decade of life, while there is decreasing prevalence among Whites in the same age category (e.g., Grant et al., 2004). These divergences in developmental paths may be due to cultural variation in education, labor market participation, drinking motives, marriage and parenting, or other factors.

1.2.1 Greek Organizations and Sexual Assaults on College Campuses

When discussing the course and consequences of binge drinking and alcohol misuse among college students and young adults, we would be remiss not to mention Greek organizations (fraternities and sororities) and alcohol-related sexual assault. Greek houses are renowned for their heavy drinking, alcohol-centric culture (Barry, 2007), and sexual assaults are an unfortunate but not uncommon byproduct of excessive alcohol consumption – especially in environments where drinking and "partying" are ubiquitous, as they are on most college campuses.

Greek Organizations
College students who are affiliated with Greek organizations (i.e., fraternities and sororities) have consistently been found to drink more heavily and experience more alcohol-related consequences than nonaffiliated students (e.g., Barry, 2007). Moreover, because of the highly social nature of Greek houses, drinking is particularly heavy among students who live in them, as opposed to those who live in dorms or in off-campus housing (Wechsler, 1996). Clinicians who begin working with college students in the Greek system should be aware that the drinking norms among these students are often higher and the pressure to binge can be greater than it is among non-Greek students (Wechsler, 1996). Fortunately, studies of brief motivational interventions for college student drinking suggest that students in Greek organizations are just as responsive to treatment as students who are not in such organizations (Murphy, Correia, Colby, & Vuchinich, 2005). Therefore, other than the treating clinician having some background information and knowledge of the drinking culture in fraternities and sororities (see Barry, 2007, for further discussion), most clinicians working with Greek students should feel as comfortable implementing

the treatments discussed in this book as they would with non-Greek college student drinkers.

Sexual Assault

Sexual assaults are common on college campuses, with at least half of the assaults involving alcohol consumption by the perpetrator, the victim, or both (e.g., Abbey, 2002). There are many possible explanations for the relationship between drinking and sexual assaults among young people – for example, getting drunk lowers inhibitions and restraint, perpetrators may drink more to have an excuse for their planned behavior, third variables such as impulsivity and peer norms may lead both to heavy drinking and higher rates of sexual assault – and it is likely that all of these and more are involved in sexual assaults on college campuses (Abbey, 2002). In recent years, sexual assaults among college students have received heightened attention by government officials (DeGue, 2014) and have become a focus of many school administrations. Because of alcohol's large role in many/most of these assaults, some evidence-based interventions now include information for potential victims regarding how to drink safely and avoid getting into risky situations, as well as information for potential perpetrators about limiting drinking, the importance of consent (and how someone cannot legally consent while intoxicated), and challenging myths about masculinity and sexual dominance (e.g., the Challenging College Alcohol Abuse interventions, summarized by National Registry of Evidence-based Programs and Practices, 2014)

1.3 Differential Diagnosis and Comorbidities

Though various signs and symptoms of psychopathology (e.g., panic attacks, delusions, mood disturbance, hallucinations, impulsivity) are often nonspecific and can reflect any of a number of conditions, SUDs and substance use, including alcohol-related disorders and other aspects of alcohol misuse, are diagnosed based on relatively specific aspects of use.

However, sometimes these "specific aspects of use" are not straightforward to assess. For example, impaired control (also known as "larger/longer") is defined in the DSM-5 as taking alcohol "in larger amounts or over a longer period than was intended" (American Psychiatric Association, 2013, p. 490). Such definitions raise the questions of "how much larger?" or "how much longer?" that can be operationalized in different ways. Moreover, the intent of the items is clearly to assess "loss of control," but careful study of individuals' interpretations of this item reveals that some drinkers, especially adolescents, respond affirmatively for other reasons (e.g., being caught up in a social function where they are being pressured to drink; Chung & Martin, 2005). Similarly, the DSM-5 defines tolerance as reflecting either increased amounts of alcohol to achieve the desired effect, or experiencing less of an effect from continued use of the same amount (APA, 2013). However, how much more alcohol is necessary to endorse this criterion? Depending on how it is operationalized, tolerance can be a frequently endorsed or relatively rarely endorsed symptom.

Although perhaps more obvious, assessing binge drinking for clinical purposes requires some attention to the details noted earlier. For individuals with large body masses, fast alcohol metabolism, and who consume their drinks over a long period of time, the five/four criteria described earlier may produce false positive results. In contrast, for individuals with small body masses, slow alcohol metabolism, and who "toss" their drinks quickly, the five/four criterion could produce false negatives. Although it is impractical to assess the alcohol metabolism rates of every individual in a typical clinical setting, obtaining detailed drinking histories, as described in the "Brief Alcohol Screening and Intervention for College Students" section during the discussion of Timeline Followback procedures (see Section 4.3.1), in conjunction with body weight and sex, allow clinicians to calculate more accurately whether and how often clients drink to intoxication (e.g., 0.08 g/dL) and whether they are drinking to levels associated with acute physical risk. In so doing, however, it must be remembered that such calculations, although more informative than using metrics like the five/four criterion, are still imprecise owing to many factors (e.g., lack of knowledge of drink size, ethanol concentration, drinking mixed drinks with considerable variability compared with beer and wine, stomach contents, individual variation in ethanol metabolism, whether the drinker vomited prior to alcohol being fully absorbed).

> Issues with the five/four binge criterion: body mass and alcohol metabolism variation, speed of consumption, and stomach contents before and during the drinking episode

1.3.1 Comorbidities

Although most of the research literature on alcohol-related comorbidity does not focus on early adulthood as a specific life stage, the general associations described in the overall adult literature should still apply. Most of the disorders

Table 3
Psychiatric Comorbidity With Alcohol Dependence

	% Nondependent population with specified disorder	% Alcohol-dependent population with specified disorder
No disorder	87.5	69.4*
Mixed anxiety disorder	6.2	9.9*
Generalized anxiety disorder	2.4	5.3*
Depression	1.2	7.3*
Phobia	0.8	1.0*
Panic disorder	0.5	2.7*

*$p < .001$.
Adapted with permission from Farrell, M., Howes, S., Bebbington, P. Brugha, T., Jenkins, R., Lewis, G. ... Meltzer, H. (2001). Nicotine, alcohol and drug dependence and psychiatric comorbidity: Results of a national household survey. *The British Journal of Psychiatry, 179*(5), p. 432–437. © 2001 by The British Journal of Psychiatry. Available at http://bjp.rcpsych.org/content/179/5/432.full

with which alcohol-related disorders are comorbid have high prevalence rates during this developmental period. Given this, it is important to note that individuals with alcohol-related disorders are more likely to exhibit another psychiatric disorder than are persons without a diagnosis, but the nature of these beyond-chance associations is difficult to assess. For example, (a) an alcohol-related disorder can be secondary to a primary psychiatric disorder; (b) a psychiatric disorder can be secondary to primary an alcohol-related disorder; (c) both disorders could arise from a common diathesis or underlying vulnerability; (d) bidirectional influence can occur; and (e) overlapping diagnostic criteria can create artifactual associations (see Sher & Trull, 1996). Notably, comorbidity rates vary according to the population sampled, the diagnostic approach employed, the specific comorbid condition under consideration, sex, and the extent of other drug use. Below, the comorbidity of AUDs with drug use disorders, mood/anxiety disorders, and personality disorders is discussed (see Table 3).

Drug Use Disorders

> Highest rates of comorbidity with AUDs occur with other substance use disorders, such as drug use disorders or tobacco dependence

Alcohol-related disorders (or more specifically, DSM AUDs, which are more commonly studied than ICD alcohol-related diagnoses) are most highly comorbid with other SUDs (e.g., drug use disorders and tobacco dependence). It should be noted that drug use disorders show a very similar epidemiological pattern to AUDs with respect to the age prevalence curve, maturing out, and rates of onset, persistence, and recurrence (Vergés et al., 2012). The co-occurrence of substance (alcohol or drug) use disorders (i.e., homotypic comorbidity) has been well documented in a number of large-scale surveys. Individuals with past 12-month drug use disorders, compared with those without such a diagnosis, have significantly higher odds of meeting criteria for an AUD (Stinson et al., 2005). The magnitude of these associations is especially noteworthy, as illustrated by the strong association between cocaine dependence and AUDs (OR [odds ratio] = 43.0). The high comorbidity among SUDs is important clinically in that it is often the case that treatment of alcohol problems is complicated by the presence of other substance use pathology. This comorbidity is also important etiologically because it suggests that there may be common causes or influences across diverse forms of SUDs. It is important to note that sociodemographic and psychopathological correlates differ between individuals who (1) only meet criteria for AUDS (AUD-only), (2) only meet criteria for drug use disorders (drug use disorder [DUD]–only), or (3) meet criteria for both AUDS and drug use disorders (comorbid AUD/DUD). Relevant to young adulthood, combined AUD/DUD comorbidity was strongly associated with being under age 30 and was also associated with substantially more treatment seeking that those with AUDs alone. Alcohol use commonly co-occurs with tobacco use. Individuals with AUDs are more likely to smoke than those without an AUD, social drinkers are more likely to smoke than nondrinkers, and individuals with tobacco use disorder exhibit greater risk for AUDs (NIAAA, 2007a). Further, concurrent alcohol and tobacco use appears to interact synergistically to produce elevated health risks (NIAAA, 2007a). For some purposes, it may be useful to consider tobacco use as an important subtyping variable when considering trajectories of alcohol misuse, in that combined drinking and smoking shows some unique associations with etiological variables and comorbidity (e.g., conduct disorder and alcohol expectancies). These findings illustrate the ability of conjoint, developmental trajectory approaches to provide information regarding AUDs' co-occurrence with other psychiatric disorders that would otherwise remain "masked" by separately examining predictors of AUDs and other disorders. Such an approach could be applied to examine AUDs' co-occurrence with other substances (e.g., marijuana) as well as other psychiatric disorders (e.g., mood/anxiety disorders, personality disorders [PDs]). It should also be noted that the profile of tobacco smoking has changed in recent years, with an increased number of smokers who report smoking intermittently (i.e., on a nondaily basis). For intermittent smokers for whom smoking appears to be highly situational, drinking alcohol can be a major discriminative stimulus for smoking.

Mood/Anxiety Disorders

As with AUDs, mood and anxiety disorders are among the most prevalent psychiatric disorders in the United States, with rates for any 12-month independent mood (e.g., major depression) and anxiety (e.g., generalized anxiety disorder [GAD]) disorders in the US population estimated at 9.2% and 11.1%, respectively (Grant et al., 2004). Moreover, AUDs and independent mood and anxiety disorders commonly co-occur. (By "independent," it is meant that the mood or anxiety disorder is not alcohol-induced [i.e., brought on by alcohol use] and its appearance is not restricted to periods of heavy drinking or their immediate aftermath.) Further, of individuals with a current AUD who sought treatment during the same period, approximately 41% and 33% had at least one current independent mood or anxiety disorder, respectively (Grant et al., 2004), suggesting that mood and anxiety disorders should be addressed by substance abuse treatment providers.

Among individuals with a current AUD diagnosis, 41% also have a mood disorder, and 33% an anxiety disorder

Note that although most population-based studies of comorbidity in adulthood do not provide rates that are specific to given age stratum, Kessler et al. (2005) derived seven classes of general comorbidity among the internalizing and externalizing disorders assessed in the National Comorbidity Survey–Replication (NCS-R) study. None of these comorbid classes was found to be more prevalent in older adults (> 30 years of age) than in younger adults (18–29 years of age); two of these comorbid classes were more prevalent in younger adults. This general pattern of findings suggests that patterns of comorbidity obtained in age-heterogeneous samples of adults likely generalize to subsamples of young adults or might, in some cases, reflect underestimates.

At least one explanation of the significant co-occurrence between alcohol-related disorders and mood/anxiety disorders are affect regulation models (see Chapter 2 "Theories and Models of Alcohol Misuse") that posit that individuals may be motivated to use alcohol to regulate negative and/or anxious emotions commonly associated with depression and anxiety. However, it should be noted that the relation between alcohol-related disorders and mood/anxiety disorders is complex, and only a fraction of individuals with alcohol-related disorders have a history of anxiety disorders. Indeed, in the NESARC data (Grant et al., 2004), only 19% and 17% of individuals with a past-year AUD were diagnosed with at least one mood and anxiety disorder, respectively. Thus, though individuals with an AUD are also more likely to be diagnosed with a mood or anxiety disorder compared with the general population, only a minority of individuals with AUDs experience a co-occurring mood/anxiety disorder, suggesting that other factors (e.g., severity of AUD, motivation for alcohol use) may contribute to the likelihood of the co-occurrence of AUDs with mood/anxiety disorders.

When assessing comorbidity between alcohol misuse and mood and anxiety problems, it is important to consider the possibility that some forms of anxiety and mood disorders appear to be "alcohol-induced," and thus, differential diagnosis of substance-induced mood disorders is considered critical for nosology and treatment (American Psychiatric Association, 2000). That is, chronic alcohol consumption can lead to affective states that resemble mood and anxiety disorders (and alcohol withdrawal is characterized by both subjective anxiety and autonomic hyperarousal similar to that seen in anxiety disorders). Anxiety and mood disorders that remit spontaneously after a short period (less than a month) of abstinence and that only appear in the context of ongoing substance use should be considered substance-induced and not "independent." However, such a determination requires a period of abstinence and may not be easily made at the outset of treatment.

Clinical Pearl
Recognizing Alcohol-Related Mood and Anxiety

Chronic alcohol misuse and overconsumption can lead people to experience altered affective states that are higher in anxiety than they might be "normally" or than they were prior to the onset of the misuse. Also, withdrawal from alcohol is often characterized by hyperarousal and increased feelings of anxiousness, so sometimes people who may appear to be acutely nervous or anxious may just be experiencing withdrawal effects from their most recent heavy drinking episode. Thus, anxiety and mood disorders that only appear within the context of perpetual misuse or recent abstention (i.e., within the past month) should be considered substance-induced, and do not necessarily require independent treatment.

It should be noted that sometimes comorbid conditions are differentiated based on whether they are primary or secondary with respect to each other – that is, according to which disorder precedes the other. Although the intent of such classification is to discern etiological precedence, such efforts can be arbitrary in that how to date the onset of each disorder is itself considerably arbitrary. For example, should we establish temporal precedence based on the age of first symptom, age at second symptom, or age when the full syndromal criteria are met? To complicate matters, studies of early adolescent substance abuse find correlations between mood states and alcohol use – that is, "comorbidity" before there is any morbidity in a formal sense. Thus, though it might be useful to be able to determine whether condition A precedes condition B or condition B precedes condition A, in practice, this can be exceedingly difficult. Moreover, two conditions can mutually influence each other, can both be caused by a third variable, or can co-occur by chance. Even in the case where one can make a strong argument based on circumstantial evidence that, let's say, an anxiety disorder "caused" an alcohol-related disorder, the "secondary" condition can become functionally autonomous, and treatment would be required for both conditions regardless of their origins.

Personality Disorders

Although several studies have examined the prevalence of PDs among individuals with alcohol-related disorders, it is only recently that data have become available that systematically document the co-occurrence of different PDs with AUDs in the general population and across different age groups. Data from NESARC (Grant et al. 2004) indicates that the co-occurrence of PDs with AUDs is pervasive in the US population. Individuals with alcohol dependence are at increased risk to also meet the diagnosis criteria for a number of PDs, especially antisocial, borderline, and narcissistic PD. The strong relation between AUDs and these disorders is not surprising, given the centrality of impulsivity to both these disorders and AUDs (see Chapter 2 "Theories and Models of Alcohol Misuse"). Although PDs are conceptualized as being relatively fixed and persistent, their symptoms can change a great deal over time, at least in early adulthood.

Most population-based studies of PDs do not break down findings by age strata. However, in a Norwegian sample, Torgersen et al. (2001) found that prevalence of PDs in early adulthood (18–29 years of age) tended to be similar to prevalence in mid-adulthood (30–49 years) and slightly lower than in late adulthood (50–65 years). Given the paucity of population-based data on this issue and for the purposes of this volume, we undertook a series of analyses of the large NESARC data set to explore the prevalence of PD in young adults (under 25). Our findings show that for nine of the 10 DSM-IV PDs assessed in NESARC, the prevalence rates were higher in young adults than in older adults; only for obsessive-compulsive personality disorder was there no age difference in prevalence. For the two PDs most commonly identified in the literature as being associated with alcohol misuse (i.e., antisocial personality disorder and borderline personality disorder), prevalence rates were approximately twice as high in younger versus older adults. This is not surprising given the clinical lore that both of these conditions tend to diminish in intensity with increased maturity. The findings are also consistent with basic research on personality change which shows that traits related to disinhibition change over the course of adulthood, especially during the third decade of life (Roberts et al., 2006). There are several models explaining the comorbidity between SUDs and PDs, with some suggesting that PDs predict the development of SUDs, and others suggesting the relationship to be the other way around. With the perspective that certain PDs reflect extreme expressions of common personality traits, recent research has posited and empirically examined drinking motives as mediators in the relation between PD symptoms and AUDs. Several studies (e.g., Tragesser, Sher, Trull, & Park, 2007) suggest that enhancement (but not coping) motives mediate the relation between AUDs and PD symptoms, especially in regard to so-called dramatic/emotional PDs such as antisocial and borderline PDs. These findings suggest that treatment of comorbid AUDs and PDs should focus both on developing strategies for positive emotion regulation/maintenance and on interventions aimed at managing features related to impulsive/sensation-seeking personality traits (Tragesser et al., 2007).

Clearly, AUDs are highly comorbid with many other conditions, and clinicians should be aware of these conditions and assess for them, as they can affect treatment planning as well as course of treatment. Most of the treatment approaches that have been specifically developed for young adults focus on the drinking itself without much consideration for other pathology. Consequently, it is important to determine the extent to which a treatment plan addresses comorbid issues, ranging from the treatment approach itself, to the setting in which it is delivered. Depending on the nature of the problem, comorbid pathology can either not be addressed directly, addressed as part of the treatment plan, or so severe in comparison with the drinking issues as to warrant referral to a provider to address the more severe condition.

1.4 Diagnostic Procedures and Documentation

The later chapter "Assessment and Treatment Indications" (see Chapter 3) will discuss a variety of assessment methods and considerations in more detail, but a brief initial review may serve as a helpful introduction.

Depending on the domain of alcohol involvement assessed, there are a number of approaches for assessing alcohol-related constructs of interest. There is a range of self-report measures that can be administered in traditional paper-and-pencil format, by computer (including interactive voice response), or by an interviewer either in-person, by phone, or by another remote telecommunication device. In addition, acute and very recent alcohol consumption can be objectively assessed by biosensors such as breath alcohol analyzers (e.g., Breathalyzers™, Intoxilyzers™), and passive transdermal ethanol sensors that can be worn on the wrist (e.g., WrisTAS™) or ankle (e.g., SCRAM™). Chronic patterns of consumption can sometimes be assessed by use of so-called biomarkers obtained from blood and include liver functions (e.g., alanine aminotransferase [ALT], aspartate aminotransferase [AST], gamma-glutamyl transpeptidase [γGT]), hematological markers (e.g., mean corpuscular volume), and carbohydrate deficient transferrin. The value of these markers in younger drinkers without extensive histories of drinking is questionable, and even in patients with long-standing histories of drinking problems, the sensitivity and specificity of these markers are less than what is desirable. However, more recently developed markers that rely on signs of oxidative damage to tissue and DNA show promise in identifying young adults with only 4–5 years of drinking experience and no evidence of liver impairment (Rendón-Ramírez, Cortés-Couto, Martínez-Rizo, Muñiz-Hernández, & Velázquez-Fernández, 2013).

Although there are clearly situations when objective monitoring of consumption using alcohol analysis devices and biomarkers are necessary, most routine practice assessment relies on language-based assessments for screening (e.g., Alcohol Use Disorders Identification Test [AUDIT]; Reinert & Allen, 2007), assessing alcohol consumption patterns (e.g., the Timeline Followback Interview [TLFB]; Agrawal, Sobell, & Sobell, 2008), alcohol consequences (e.g., Rutgers Alcohol Problem Index [RAPI]; Neal, Corbin, & Fromme, 2006), alcohol expectancies (e.g., Comprehensive Effects of Alcohol; Fromme, Stroot, & Kaplan, 1993; Ham et al., 2005), reasons for drinking/drinking motivations (e.g., Drinking Motives Questionnaire-Revised [DMQ-R]; Cooper, 1994; psychometrically evaluated for use in undergraduate college students by Grant, Stewart, O'Connor, Blackwell, & Conrod, 2007), readiness and motivation to change (Heather, Smailes, & Cassidy, 2008), and diagnostic interviews. In addition, structured and semistructured interviews have been developed for both lay interviewers and trained clinicians. Many of these instruments (as well as others) can be evaluated and downloaded from the Project PhenX website (https://www.phenx.org/). The assessment instruments in the PhenX Substance Abuse and Addiction (SAA) Project represent a useful collection of scales and interviews that have been accepted by the field, are well documented, and are nonproprietary (at least those in the substance use collection).

In addition, there has been increased interest in using various types of electronic diaries to record drinking events (e.g., the nature and number of drinks, drinking contexts) in real time using smartphones (and previously, personal digital assistants [PDAs]). Until recently, this type of technology was used primarily in research contexts, but with the proliferation of smartphones in recent years, more and more apps to track drinking are becoming available and are used easily within clinical contexts as self-monitoring "homework" (perhaps in lieu of paper-and-pencil self-monitoring worksheets) to be reviewed during in-person sessions.

2

Theories and Models of Alcohol Misuse

Major models of alcohol misuse: pharmacological vulnerability, behavioral undercontrol, and affect regulation

There are a number of models of alcohol misuse reflecting the large range of contributing factors to problem drinking. Although these can be defined in a number of ways, they can be broadly conceived as reflecting pharmacological vulnerability to the drug ethanol, behavioral undercontrol (or externalizing behavior), and affect regulation. It should be noted that these general classes of models are not necessarily in competition – rather, they account for different sources of influences on drinking and relate to different aspects of drinking motivation. In a given case, multiple models may be relevant because risk factors for these different models and underlying processes are conceptually distinct but related. Moreover, each of these broad classes of models is composed of different submodels.

Although we will use the above framework for highlighting different theories and models of drinking behavior, it should be noted that such a framework encompasses so-called dual-process models, which have gained currency in recent years, especially with respect to alcohol misuse. There are many dual-process models that are fundamentally similar in the sense that all posit that alcohol misuse reflects an imbalance between two opposing "processes" associated with approach tendencies to drink and restraining tendencies that can inhibit approach, an "impulsive system" related to the seeking of immediate rewards and a reflective system concerned with longer term rewards and values (e.g., Bechara, 2005). Within these models, the impulsive system is likely to be automatic and, at least in part, outside of conscious awareness. This is in contrast to other models that basically view alcohol (and other substance) use as a primarily rational process (e.g., Kuther, 2002). It should be noted, however, that these kinds of prototypic distinctions are somewhat crude generalizations in that highly practiced "reflective" behaviors can become automatized, and individuals are sometimes aware of their own impulsive processes. Regardless, the notion that alcohol misuse represents an imbalance between restraining tendencies and approach tendencies is a very useful one both for organizing the research literature and for providing a conceptual framework for clinicians to consider multiple avenues for interventions with drinkers (e.g., targeting approach processes vs. targeting restraint processes).

However, before considering models of alcohol misuse, it is useful to briefly review the stated reasons for drinking that drinkers provide. Although dual-process models suggest that drinkers may not be fully aware of their reasons for dinking, to the extent that there is a conscious aspect to drinking, and/or drinkers can infer their own motives, this research is informative. The best-established framework for understanding self-reported drinking motives is the one proposed by Lynne Cooper (1994) in a study of adolescent and adult drinkers. Cooper found that the assessment of the factor structure of stated reasons for drinking yields a reliable multidimensional, four-factor structure: (1) social motives (e.g., "to be sociable"), (2) enhancement motives (e.g., "to get high," "because it's fun"), (3) coping motives (e.g., "to forget your worries," "because it helps when you feel depressed or nervous"), and (4) conformity motives (e.g., "to fit in") – see Table 4. Notably, enhancement and coping motives (but not social or conformity motives) are strongly associated with drinking, heavy drinking, and drinking problems in both adolescence and adulthood, which points to somewhat specific motivational pathways arising from individual differences that relate to the affect regulation pathways described next. However, there is some debate in the literature as to whether we can effectively divide drinkers into distinct groups of those who drink for either (1) enhancement motives or (2) coping motives, or whether these motivational domains are better viewed as continuous and multivariate, with most drinkers being versatile in their motivation (Littlefield, Vergés, Rosinski, Steinley, & Sher, 2013).

Table 4
Drinking Motives

Type of motive	Example	Associations
Social	To be sociable, to be friendlier	
Enhancement	To have more fun, to get high	Heavy drinking, drinking problems, extraversion
Coping	To forget your worries, to feel less anxious	Heavy drinking, drinking problems, neuroticism
Conformity	Because everyone else is, to fit in	

2.1 Affect Regulation

Affect regulation models of alcohol use and misuse refer to both *negative affect regulation* (i.e., drinking to relieve negative affect, negative reinforcement) and *positive affect regulation* (i.e., drinking to induce positive mood states, positive reinforcement), which correspond to what Cooper (1994) described as coping and enhancement motivations, respectively. There are a number of specific submodels of negative affective regulation that scientists have proposed. Although all posit that alcohol is consumed to regulate emotions, the models differ in the extent to which various parameters influence whether, and the extent to which, alcohol will reduce negative affect and under what conditions negative affective states will motivate drinking. Such parameters include dose, the temporal relationship between negative affect and alcohol consumption, the degree of cognitive mediation of alcohol effects, the nature of the negative affective states, and underlying approach–avoidance

> Affect regulation models emphasize the role of negative affective states in the onset and maintenance of alcohol use problems

dynamics. For the clinician conceptualizing a specific case, the importance of this general model is that it suggests that aversive subjective states should be assessed and considered as potentially important to the etiology and maintenance of the drinking problem. Should it appear that drinking is being motivated by negative affective states, alternative primary and secondary (emotion-focused) coping should be assessed and considered as a focus of treatment. Support for theories of negative affect regulation models come from multiple data sources and defy a simple summary. However, there is little question that under the right circumstances, alcohol can strongly reduce negative emotions and increase positive emotions.

It is important to emphasize that chronic, heavy alcohol consumption can induce negative affect, spurring further drinking that might provide short-term relief from negative affect but contribute to continued if not worsened negative affect in general. Major theories of alcohol dependence (e.g., Baker, Piper, McCarthy, Majeskie, & Fiore, 2004) posit that it is this chasing of relief from dependence-induced negative affect that drives continued drinking and is at the heart of addiction to alcohol. For clinicians, it emphasizes the need not only to assess negative affectivity in their clients but also to determine whether and how much this negative affectivity is a consequence of consumption rather than an independent risk factor. In addition to assessing drinking motives via measures like the DMQ-R, assessing those situations that tend to trigger emotions that increase the likelihood of drinking with tools such as the Brief Situational Confidence Questionnaire (BSCQ; Breslin, Sobell, Sobell, & Agrawal, 2000) can help identify high-risk situations for alcohol misuse that could be the focus of treatment. It should be noted that typologies of alcoholism that have identified various subtypes routinely find that those types associated with negative affectivity tend to have later onsets and characterize older persons with drinking problems. This suggests that negative affect regulation, although important over the life span, maybe be relatively less important in young adulthood than some of the other models of drinking.

Although coping motivated drinking is more directly associated with drinking problems than enhancement drinking, enhancement drinking and thus positive affect regulation drinking appear to be more common and more strongly associated with heavy consumption, especially in younger adults. Measures like the DMQ-R and the BSCQ can assess those self-perceptions of reward seeking as a drinking motive, as well as perceived self-efficacy at controlling drinking in situations characterized by drinking for positive reinforcement. Thus, a primary drinking motivation in this population is "to get buzzed" or to "get drunk." Like all drugs of abuse, alcohol is known to have strong effects on mesolimbic dopamine pathways, a critical neurocircuit associated with positive reinforcement. This model is likely most clearly relevant for individuals high in reward seeking and related traits such as novelty seeking and sensation seeking, which are well-established risk factors for drinking and drinking problems at this stage of life as well as more generally. Such traits can be measured by a range of personality trait measures that assess various aspects of self-control. One such useful measure for clinicians is the UPPS-P (Cyders et al., 2007), which assesses five distinct traits related to impulsivity, including sensation seeking, negative affect urgency, premeditation, perseverance, and positive urgency. Not surprisingly, personality traits associated with sensation seeking are correlated with enhancement motives. To the clinician, this model provides a context for understanding that enhancement motives reflect more than the neuropharmacological properties of the drug ethanol and can be deeply rooted temperamentally. That is, the positive reinforcement from alcohol serves basic personal needs, so effective treatment will include getting those excessive needs for positive reinforcement met in alternative and, hopefully, less harmful ways. To address this issue, some clinical research programs have developed treatment programs directly targeting these underlying traits. For example, Conrod et al. (2013) developed different intervention approaches for students who are at high risk for alcohol misuse by virtue of their scores on measures of anxiety sensitivity, hopelessness, impulsivity, and sensation seeking. From the perspective of affect regulation models, anxiety sensitivity and hopelessness traits are most associated with negative affect regulation, and sensation-seeking traits with positive affect regulation. (Impulsivity, although clearly related to all models of alcohol use, is most closely associated with externalizing behavior and behavioral undercontrol.)

2.2   Behavioral Undercontrol

The behavioral undercontrol/externalizing model views alcohol misuse as a specific manifestation of a broader pattern of externalizing behavior characterized by rule-breaking, impulsive, and unconventional behavior. Although this model can function synergistically with affect regulation models, the behavioral undercontrol/externalizing model uniquely focuses on deficient reflective processes (e.g., poor executive function such as planning and response inhibition). The fact that a variety of problem behaviors (including alcohol use) occurs during adolescence and has common correlates is well known across cultures. In adults, factor-analytic studies of psychiatric disorders typically reveal two broad factors: internalizing disorders and externalizing disorders (e.g., Krueger, Helzer, & Hudziak, 2002). Additionally, this model appears to account for much of the variance in alcohol misuse as evidenced by the strong association between childhood externalizing disorders (such as conduct disorder and attention deficit/hyperactivity disorder) and subsequent alcohol misuse, with much of this variance associated with shared genetic influence (Edwards & Kendler, 2012).

The core constructs at the heart of behavioral undercontrol/externalizing are related to impulsivity, but it is important to emphasize that contemporary psychological research has shown us that the general term *impulsivity* refers to a number of different constructs that are conceptually and empirically distinct. As noted above, in the self-report domain, there are at least five distinct traits associated with impulsivity or a tendency to "rash action": (1) negative affect urgency, (2) positive affect urgency, (3) lack of deliberation/planning, (4) lack of persistence, and (5) sensation seeking (Cyders et al., 2007). In the behavioral domain, impulsivity is assessed with a variety of tasks including those related to the inability to inhibit pre-potent responses, susceptibility to distractor interference, susceptibility to proactive interference, distortions in elapsed time, and difficulty in delaying response (Dick et al., 2010). Difficulty

People who are low in behavioral control may appear to be aggressive, aversive to routine, need more stimulation than others, and lack an ability to constrain or inhibit their impulses

Types of impulsivity: negative affect urgency (when in a bad mood), positive affect urgency (when in a good mood), lack of deliberation/ planning, lack of persistence, and sensation seeking

in delaying responses (when there is a bias toward choosing smaller immediate rewards over delayed rewards) or "delay discounting" (where the value of delayed rewards are discounted) has been shown to be a strong correlate of substance use problems (Dick et al., 2010). Although the association between different facets of impulsivity (both within and, especially, across domains) is often quite modest, undercontrolled behavior associated with the externalizing spectrum can be viewed as reflecting at least one of these factors. Characterizing the specific nature of the deficits facing young adults with alcohol misuse can help clinicians tailor their interventions to the specific needs of their clients. It should be noted that the frontal lobes of humans continue to develop into the 20s and that some degree of maturing out of alcohol misuse appears to be associated with normative declines in impulsivity likely attributable to endogenous brain changes induced, in part, by the assumption of adult roles. Consequently, treatment approaches that promote adult socialization and training in executive functions may help to reduce alcohol problems.

2.3 Pharmacological Vulnerability

Pharmacological vulnerability models suggest that drinkers' different levels of sensitivity to alcohol contribute to their varying levels of risk for the development of alcohol problems

The pharmacological vulnerability model asserts that individual differences in the psychopharmacological effects of alcohol convey risk for alcohol misuse and dependence. Though risk was originally conceived as being reflected by one end of the sensitivity dimension, with those with relatively low sensitivity to alcohol effects being at higher risk, it was later recognized that both ends of the sensitivity dimension might be associated with risk. That is, risk for alcohol problems is associated with increased sensitivity to stimulating effects of alcohol when blood alcohol levels are rising (i.e., the ascending limb of the blood alcohol curve) and to decreased sensitivity to sedating effects when blood alcohol levels are falling (i.e., the descending limb) (see Quinn & Fromme, 2011, for a review).

> **Clinical Pearl**
> **Ascending and Descending Limbs of the BAC Curve**
>
> It may be useful to discuss with clients the ascending and descending limbs of the BAC curve, and their associated effects, to help increase their awareness of certain risks and vulnerabilities within a given drinking episode. Specifically, reviewing with clients that the ascending limb is associated with feelings of stimulation and energy, while the descending limb is associated with feelings of sluggishness and sedation, could help them recognize these effects in themselves and modify their own drinking habits. By spacing out drinks instead of chugging them or "front-loading" early in the evening, for example, drinkers' BAC curves will remain in the ascending limb for a longer period of time, and the descending limb will not be as steep or intense. This allows people to experience more of the positive stimulating effects of alcohol and fewer of the negative sedating effects. Another important point to communicate to clients about the BAC curve is that levels of subjective intoxication tend to differ on opposing ends of the curve, even when BACs are equal. For example, when on the ascending limb at a BAC of 0.08 g/dL, drinkers may feel quite buzzed and state that they would not feel comfortable

> behind the wheel of a car. However, by the time they reach 0.08 g/dL on the descending limb of the curve, this same BAC is associated with a much lower level of subjective intoxication, leading drinkers to think they are "pretty sober," in control, and fully capable of driving even though their level of cognitive impairment is just as significant as it was on the way up the curve.

There are self-report scales that can be used to assess sensitivity, and it has been suggested that at least one of these scales, the Self-Ratings of the Effects of Alcohol (SRE; Schuckit et al., 1997), can be used in applied settings to help provide normative feedback to clients on their drinking vulnerabilities. Note that providing normative feedback on variables related to drinking behavior and consequences, such as number of drinks consumed on a drinking day, maximum number of drinks consumed in a given period of time, and harmful alcohol-related outcomes, is a key component of many interventions for alcohol misuse in young adults. Providing feedback on individual differences in sensitivity to alcohol, using scales such as the SRE, can highlight unique vulnerabilities that a given drinker might have and personalize feedback to an even greater degree than those based on manifest behavior. More generally, models of pharmacological vulnerability remind clinicians of the high degree of variability in alcohol reactivity so they can consider this in their work with clients on drinking planning. For example, this theoretical perspective highlights the value of slowing down the rate of drinking (a well-established protective drinking strategy) as sensitivity to ethanol, especially the reinforcing, stimulating effects, appears to be strongly associated with the rate of change of blood alcohol on the ascending limb. It also potentially can help the drinker reframe low sensitivity as a personal risk factor for drinking that warrants a cautious approach to drinking as opposed to a "badge of honor" for being able to "hold ones liquor." In fact, it has recently been documented that some young drinkers deliberately induce tolerance by "training" for heavy drinking events through planned increases in their consumption leading up to the event (Martinez et al., 2010), and this practice is associated with more problem drinking. Helping clients view low sensitivity or high tolerance as risk factors rather than social assets represents a potentially novel approach for reassessing oneself as a drinker.

3

Assessment and Treatment Indications

Before starting treatment or an intervention with a heavy drinking young adult, it is important to fully assess the nature of the presenting problem(s). This chapter outlines some of the most empirically supported and widely used assessment tools to aid clinicians during assessment and treatment planning.

3.1 General Issues

3.1.1 Self-Report Measures

Although it was long believed that individuals (especially heavy drinkers and those with alcohol dependence) are not honest when reporting their drinking history, research has shown that self-reports of alcohol use and related constructs tend to be reliable and valid. This conclusion is based on studies comparing self-reports with collateral reports from friends or family (e.g., Connors & Maisto, 2003). This is especially true when there is a climate of trust between the client and therapist engendered by confidentiality and the absence of negative consequences (e.g., compulsory treatment, expulsion from school) for reporting alcohol use of any amount or stigmatized related behavior (e.g., drunk driving). Consequently, clinicians should have a reasonable amount of confidence in the reliability and validity of drinking-related assessments, provided these measures are completed in an interpersonal and institutional context that is conducive to valid reporting (e.g., with client sobriety and assurance of confidentiality).

3.1.2 Assessment Types and Options

Although all of the measures described in this chapter are designed to be self-reports, the types of formats employed can vary depending on the goals of the clinical assessment. For example, some measures are designed to be brief and appropriate for screening in busy clinical settings and to be quickly self-administered. Others are quite detailed and lengthy and might require special training for them to be validly administered. There is no "standard" clinical battery for clinicians to use, and the choice of measure(s) can be based on the goals of the assessment, resources available (including clinician and client time), and the emerging clinical picture. In this section, a variety of types of assessment are introduced. In addition to outlining the general utility and goals of different assessments (e.g., Why is it important to assess alcohol consequences? Why would clients' reasons for drinking have anything to do with their plan for cutting back?), specific, empirically supported examples for different types of assessment are discussed in detail. Among the types of assessments covered in this section are (a) *screening measures* (brief self-administered inventories of a drinker's general level of risk); (b) *measures of alcohol consumption* (providing information about quantity, frequency, and patterns of use); (c) *measures of alcohol-related consequences* (documenting the specific types of harms that clients have experienced as a result of drinking): (d) *diagnostic interviews* (formally assessing the presence of AUDs according to clinical criteria); (e) *measures of alcohol expectancies* (what drinkers *think* happens as a result of intoxication); (f) *drinking motives* (reasons people give for wanting to drink); and (g) *readiness to change* (clients' beliefs about their drinking problem and their willingness to make positive changes). The chapter ends with a discussion of some additional factors to consider when planning a course of treatment, such as clients' mental and physical health problems (both past and present) and treatment history. This section is intended to provide the necessary background and guidance about the assessment tools that clinicians should have as they approach the sometimes delicate course of treatment with alcohol-abusing young adults.

Screening Measures

Screening tools, intended to be brief and broad measures of alcohol use and consequences, quickly provide clinicians with useful information to inform the course of treatment. Especially in medical settings such as primary or urgent care clinics, symptoms of risky drinking and AUDs often go unnoticed, making the routine use of brief screening tools an effective and efficient way to recognize those in need of treatment, even when they may be presenting with unrelated concerns. For clinicians with their own practice or who are otherwise outside of primary or urgent care settings, a brief screening measure completed during a client's preintake session paperwork can be invaluable. A brief assessment of a person's recent drinking and related consequences can give clinicians a head start before sitting down with a new client. Of the many available alcohol-screening measures, a few are very commonly used. One of the most widely used is the AUDIT (Reinert & Allen, 2007; see Appendix 1), a 10-item measure that briefly assesses an individual's amount of alcohol use as well as the presence of dependence symptoms (e.g., needing a drink first thing in the morning) and hazardous use (e.g., experiencing alcohol-related injuries). Although scores range from 0 to 40, scores of 8 or more are "suggestive" of an alcohol problem, and should be followed up with a formal diagnostic evaluation. Several shorter versions of the 10-item AUDIT have been evaluated and found to be psychometrically sound (Reinert & Allen, 2007). The most popular, the AUDIT-C, consists of three questions that focus solely on consumption, including a gender-specific binge drinking question. Although the AUDIT and AUDIT-C provide clinicians with a brief, psychometrically sound screening option, a single question related to the frequency of heavy drinking or binge drinking (i.e., "How often in the past 30 days have you drank 4 (females)/5(males) or more drinks on one occasion?") has been found to be significantly associated with college students' reported experience of alcohol-related problems (Wechsler, Lee, Kuo, & Lee, 2000). As discussed in the next section, many brief consumption measures can also be used as screening measures. The reason that brief screening measures are recommended is that they can be scanned quickly to get an initial impression of a person's overall level of use and risk.

Consumption Measures

When working with young adults who engage in risky heavy drinking, a careful assessment of their alcohol use and related consequences is a sine qua non. In particular, it will be helpful in understanding a person's drinking patterns, including quantity, drinks per occasion, and frequency of drinking at various levels. Each of these aspects of drinking is important individually, but they take on greater significance when considered as an ensemble. For example, all other things being equal, drinking more is often associated with greater harm than drinking less often. However, all things are seldom equal. Someone can drink one or two drinks a day every day and never exceed what is considered a harmful level of consumption (men: ≤ 4 drinks on any single day and ≤ 14 drinks per week; women: ≤ 3 drinks on any single day and ≤ 7 drinks per week; NIAAA, 2007b) while someone else could drink only occasionally, but do so at a level likely to be associated with harm.

Depending on the clinical context and needs of the practitioner, drinking patterns and variability can be assessed with a variety of screening measures. Although there are several very brief measures, more detailed measures that take more time can provide both clinicians and clients with an in-depth understanding of high-risk situation(s) related to heavy drinking.

The most detailed approach to assessing drinking patterns involves having the client complete a retrospective drinking diary, known as the TLFB (Agrawal, Sobell, & Sobell, 2008). The TLFB asks clients to identify a specific time period (e.g., past month, past 90 days) during which they drank alcohol and the number of drinks consumed on each drinking day. To aid in the recall process, clients can use memory aids such as their smartphone calendar and can include personal events with friends or family (e.g., Jesse's birthday party, Spring Break) and as well as holidays (e.g., graduation, Christmas).

Though the TLFB was originally designed as an in-person interview (to allow for follow-up questions, probing for exact amounts, etc.), more user-friendly reliable formats have evolved (e.g., computerized, group-based, mail, Web-based, shorter time frames). The psychometric properties of the TLFB, including shorter and alternative formats, have been evaluated extensively for use in clinical settings (e.g., Agrawal, Sobell, & Sobell, 2008). The TLFB is currently the most psychometrically sound retrospective self-report method for assessing alcohol use. Shorter versions (30 and 60 days vs. 360 days) are recommended for use in clinical practice (Vakili, Sobell, Sobell, Simco, & Agrawal, 2008).

Another empirically supported and commonly used brief measure of alcohol consumption, the Quick Drinking Screen (QDS; Roy et al., 2008), consists of four questions and can be completed in a few minutes. The four questions inquire about a drinker's (a) average number of drinking days per week, (b) average number of drinks per occasion, (c) frequency of binge drinking (4+ females / 5+ males), and (d) maximum number of drinks consumed on any one day in the last 12 months. The QDS has been found to collect remarkably similar drinking data to the TLFB, and thus, when it is not possible for clinicians to collect detailed drinking data, the QDS provides a quick and informative measure of alcohol consumption.

3.1.3 Alcohol-Related Consequences Measures

Integral to the assessment and treatment of alcohol misuse are measures of alcohol-related consequences and problems, as well as the discussion of those consequences within the therapeutic setting. A consequence measure asks individuals to report the type and frequency of problems that they experience as a result of their drinking (e.g., blackouts, arrests, fights). Consequences can often reflect the severity of the person's alcohol use. The ways in which drinkers' alcohol use affects their friendships, schoolwork, job, familial relationships, and other aspects of their life can be helpful in understanding the seriousness of their use. This may be particularly true for young adults who are at a stage in life when alcohol consumption is unlikely to have resulted in chronic health problems. This is not to say that young-adult drinking is without health risks. In fact, heavy drinking even in the absence of immediate health consequences is viewed as risky because health problems often develop over the course of many years.

> **Sometimes assessing an individual's "average" consumption is less clinically useful than assessing their peak consumption, or exact consumption on certain days**

Clinical Pearl
Identifying and Talking About Negative Consequences

Sometimes a young-adult client will, at first, report that his or her frequent drinking is not "harming anyone" or having any ill effects. It is important for clinicians not to directly challenge that assumption, especially at the beginning of treatment when the therapeutic rapport is still developing. As the conversation about the client's drinking progresses, often information about alcohol's negative effects will slowly and subtly emerge (e.g., *"I was really hungover that Sunday and my girlfriend was pretty mad at me because I couldn't go to her family's house for lunch"*). When moments like these present themselves, follow up with the client about how that felt and, in this example, how the other party may have felt when it was happening. Then, a simple reflection might be useful to highlight that this area of the client's life is indeed negatively affected by heavy drinking, at least on occasion (*"So when we talked earlier it sounded like your drinking wasn't really causing any problems whatsoever, but from what we just talked about it sounds like it causes some fights with your girlfriend sometimes. Would you say that's accurate?"*).

Measures that assess consequences of drinking can provide clinicians and clients with valuable information that can be used as feedback during the therapeutic process. For many clients, simply completing a measure of alcohol consequences may be beneficial in that it allows them to recognize the ways alcohol has affected their lives and may serve as a motivator in the future (i.e., it might help them realize when they are getting into a situation that might be negative). In addition, when clients complete a consequence questionnaire during a session, it can provide a natural opportunity for clinicians to review and discuss their answers, thereby making the consequences more personal and important than if the item responses were collected without comment. Not going over the measure might also lead clients to take future assessments less seriously or see them as pointless, because the way they respond does not seem to affect what is being discussed in therapy.

There are many published measures for assessing alcohol consequences in young adults, the most common are (a) the RAPI (Neal, Corbin, & Fromme, 2006); (b) the Young Adult Alcohol Problems Screening Test (YAAPST; reviewed by Kahler et al., 2004); (c) the Young Adult Alcohol Consequences Questionnaire (YAACQ; Read, Kahler, & Strong, 2006); and (d) the Brief Young Adult Alcohol Consequences Questionnaire (BYAACQ; Kahler, Strong, & Read, 2005) – see Table 5. The RAPI, consisting of 23 items rated on a 5-point scale, was designed for adolescents but has been widely used with college students. Clients are asked to indicate the number of times they have experienced a certain consequence (e.g., 1–2 times, 3–4 times) within a given time frame (e.g., past month, past year). Though high scores have been found to be associated with constructs such as heavy drinking, some have suggested that the RAPI is not ideal for young-adult assessement because it was developed for non-college-age adolescents, and thus does not contain items pertaining to frequently experienced alcohol-related problems among college students and young adults (e.g., regretted sexual encounters, drunk driving). In contrast, the YAAPST (originally 27 items but expanded to 36 items, including items pertaining to regrettable sexual experiences and driving while intoxicated) was designed specifically for the assessment of alcohol problems among college students, and contains varying response options across items that differ in severity. In addition to specific frequency options (e.g., 1–2 times within the past year), all response options include *Never experienced*, *Experienced but not within the past year*, and *Experienced within the past year*. This allows clinicians to view and score responses in a variety of ways. For example, clients who reported upwards of 10 negative consequences, none of which occurred in the past year, would present with a different (i.e., less disordered) clinical profile than clients who reported the same number of consequences, but all within the past year. In the first case, clients are showing signs of reducing their harm (e.g., fewer drinking days, spacing drinks out, not drinking during high-risk situations), whereas clients in the second case show little or no evidence of practicing similar behavioral precautions to minimize their risk. This type of insight can be very useful when clinicians are trying to conceptualize a broad clinical picture with a client. Finally, the YAACQ and BYAACQ are relatively new measures that were also designed specifically for use with college students, and these represent a combination of author-developed items and items from other scales (e.g., the YAAPST). The YAACQ uses a 48-item scale, including alcohol problems related to eight subdomains: social/interpersonal consequences, impaired control, self-perception, self-care, risk behaviors, academic/occupational concerns, physical dependence, and blackout drinking. In contrast, the BYAACQ, with 24 items, is intended to reflect a single dimension of alcohol misuse. The YAACQ was developed to be sensitive to a wide range of alcohol-related harms, and is considered a comprehensive measure of consequences in college students among clinicians who have the time to use a longer scale and are interested in collecting information across multiple behavioral areas.

Table 5
Consequences Measures for Young Adults

Scale	Target population	Format
Rutgers Alcohol Problem Index (RAPI)	Adolescents & college students	23 items on a 5-point scale
Young Adult Alcohol Consequences Questionnaire (YAAPST)	College students	27 or 36 items with varying response options depending on item severity
Young Adult Alcohol Consequences Questionnaire (YAACQ)	College students	48 items with eight subdomains
Brief Young Adult Alcohol Consequences Questionnaire (BYAACQ)	College students	24 items reflecting a single dimension of alcohol misuse

3.2 Diagnosing an Alcohol Use Disorder

Although it is rare that formal diagnostic information would alter the course of treatment, some clinicians might want or need to conduct such assessments for reasons related to institutional policy (e.g., they might be required by clinics or hospitals and/or for third-party reimbursement). Specifically, as of October of 2015, insurance companies will require ICD diagnostic codes for billing purposes and no longer accept DSM codes (APA Practice Organization – Practice Central, 2014). This will result in many clinicians (who were trained on the DSM) learning to assess and diagnose based on ICD criteria (although, because ICD codes are now included in the DSM-5 next to the corresponding disorders, the American Psychological Association encourages clinicians "to use the criteria as outlined in the DSM-5 to arrive at diagnostic conclusions and then use the appropriate ICD code set for billing purposes" [APA Practice Organization – Practice Central, 2014]). To assess for the presence of alcohol-related disorders, an in-person structured or semistructured interview can be helpful, though some self-completed checklists can also be used. (For a detailed discussion of the criterion for alcohol-related diagnoses in the DSM-5 and ICD-10, please see Subsection 1.1.4 titled "Diagnosis," in Section 1.1 "Terminology and Definitions").

To assess for the presence of ADS or harmful use (according to ICD-10 criteria), or a mild, moderate, or severe AUD (according to DSM-5 criteria), trained clinicians can choose to administer the WHO World Mental Health (WMH) Survey Initiative version of the Composite International Diagnostic Interview (WHO WMH-CIDI; Kessler & Üstün, 2004) for ICD-10 diagnoses, or the Structured Clinical Interview for DSM Disorders (SCID; First, Williams, Karg, & Spitzer, 2014) for DSM-5 diagnoses. Both assess for the presence of mood and psychotic disorders as well as alcohol and substance-related disorders. To assess for ADS or harmful use, clinicians should use the WHO WMH-CIDI, which is a standardized diagnostic assessment of mental disorders based on the criteria and definitions of the ICD-10. (Note that the WHO WMH-CIDI also contains criteria necessary to make DSM-IV diagnoses, but these are increasingly obsolete with the publication of the DSM-5 and adoption of ICD-10 coding). The WHO WMH-CIDI contains a detailed substance abuse module that provides information on the quality and severity of an individual's problems with tobacco, alcohol, and nine categories of illicit drugs. Because it is a *structured* assessment, it includes enough specificity to be used by individuals who are trained in the administration of the test but do not have a clinical background. If a clinician is interested in making a DSM-5 diagnosis, however, he or she should administer the SCID, which is a semistructured (as opposed to structured) interview. Because it is semistructured, the format is less rigid and more flexible than structured interviews such as the WHO WMH-CIDI, so only those with appropriate clinical training should administer it, since probing, clarification, and further exploration are often necessary.

Because diagnostic interviews are designed to produce categorical decisions (i.e., a person does or does not have an AUD), they commonly have suboptimal reliability, especially for people who *barely* meet the criteria or who are near the diagnostic threshold (Grant et al., 2004). In particular, diagnostic assessments with young-adult populations have demonstrated even lower levels of reliability, due to certain items being applied differently to this age group, or interviewees' misinterpreting the meaning of the items. Regarding the former, the criterion of *tolerance* can be confusing. One item within this criterion is the need *to drink a lot more in order to get the feeling they wanted than they did when they first started drinking* (this is the item from the SCID for DSM-5). Though this may be an indicator of recent heightened drinking and physiological dependence for a person in their 40s who has been drinking at low levels for 20 years, for someone who is 19 and has been drinking for less than a year, this item may reflect the nonpathological tolerance that comes with consuming alcohol for the first time. In such cases, clinicians may need to use their best judgment about whether a client's response truly meets the spirit of the item of increased tolerance. In addition, as noted above, young clients may misinterpret the nature of an item and this can lead to false positive responses. For example, as noted earlier, many young people have been found to meet criteria for *drinking in larger amounts or for longer periods of time than intended,* not because of a loss of control or compulsion, which the item is designed to assess, but because of social or circumstantial reasons (e.g., playing a drinking game; Chung & Martin, 2005). Because of concerns like these, as well as other nuances that emerge when applying diagnostic criteria to young people, it is important for clinicians to be familiar with the specific nature of all criteria when performing a clinical interview so as to be able to ask the right questions, as well as to assess a range of other variables related to a drinker's alcohol and drug use, general health, and psychiatric and medical history, before determining the best course of treatment for a young adult with an alcohol problem.

3.3 Other Assessment Domains

Beyond aspects of consumption, consequences, and certain symptoms that may or may not meet formal diagnostic status, there are other domains that might be helpful for clinicians to assess before treatment starts. For example, assessing clients' motivation to change their drinking and how confident they are that they can make those changes can provide valuable insights into the best ways to progress with treatment. In addition, if useful feedback is provided, brief assessments about topics such as why clients drink and what they hope to experience as a result of drinking, how open they are to cutting back, etc., can serve as interventions themselves (Carey, Carey, Henson, Maisto, & DeMartini, 2011). Providing information to clients about their drinking and related consequences can serve as an opportunity to discuss their drinking in an open and supportive environment and even be a catalyst for self-change.

3.4 Expectancies

Assessing and understanding alcohol expectancies (AOEs) or the effects that an individual anticipates from drinking are key factors in most cognitive behavioral treatment programs. AOEs have been found to be related to drinkers' moods and behaviors when intoxicated, their treatment success and relapse rates, and other key variables associated with problem and nonproblem drinking. Positive alcohol outcome expectancies (also called alcohol expectancies; e.g., I'm more social when I'm drunk) have been associated with poorer treatment outcomes, whereas negative alcohol outcome expectancies (e.g., I get nauseated when I'm drunk) have been associated with better treatment outcomes (though the evidence has been mixed; see Jones, Corbin, & Fromme, 2001, for a review). For clinicians, assessing and discussing clients' alcohol expectancies within a supportive, nonjudgmental, and therapeutic context can help clients become more aware of what they think happens as a result of drinking, as well as the ways in which alcohol use often does not meet those expectations (Jones, 2004). As will be discussed in the chapter "Treatment" (see Chapter 4), addressing the accuracy of clients' positive alcohol expectancies can help lead to a reduction in the strength of the belief in those expectancies. In fact, the assessment, feedback, and discussion of AOEs have been considered so fundamental in the treatment of young-adult alcohol misuse that the NIAAA recommended these components be included in interventions when the College Drinking Task Force published its recommendations in 2002 (Malloy, Goldman, & Kington, 2002).

One commonly used measure of alcohol expectancies is the Comprehensive Effects of Alcohol (CEOA; Fromme, Stroot, & Kaplan, 1993), which has been psychometrically evaluated in undergraduate college students by Ham, Stewart, Norton, and Hope (2005). Unlike other expectancy scales, the CEOA assesses both positive (e.g., I would be friendly) and negative (e.g., I would feel moody) expectancies. The measure contains two main parts, the first an assessment of AOEs (beginning with the stem, If I were under the influence from drinking alcohol…[e.g., I would be clumsy], rated on a 4-point Likert scale from 1 = *disagree* to 4 = *agree*), followed by subjective evaluation ratings of the effects, on a 5-point Likert scale (1 = *bad,* 3 = *neutral,* 5 = *good).* Levels of positive and negative alcohol expectancies and subjective evaluations assessed through the CEOA have been found to account for significant variability in drinking and alcohol-related health problems, making it a valuable clinical tool for use through the assessment and treatment process. Notably, this measure is often used in clinical practice without the evaluative component, and it is still very useful.

Clinicians seeing young-adult binge drinkers might want to consider assessing and discussing their clients' responses to this measure early in treatment in order to obtain a sense of their views of the immediate benefits and harms associated with drinking. After this initial assessment, clinicians should (gently, and without judgment or criticism) discuss their clients' alcohol expectancies and how they match up with their real-life experiences. For example, a clinician could say something like: "*I see that you strongly believe that if you were under the influence of alcohol you would feel both peaceful and relaxed. In thinking about the last couple of times you've been intoxicated, how relaxed and peaceful did you feel*?"

3.5 Drinking Motives

Measures of drinking motives assess the reasons drinkers are driven or motivated to drink alcohol. Although drinking motives may at first appear to be the same as alcohol expectancies, motives focus on *why people want to drink*, whereas expectancies refer to *what people believe happens as a result of drinking*. In fact, a drinker might hold certain expectancies and never actually drink for those reasons, or they might even be motivated *not* to drink because of them. For example, if a young woman expects to become more sexually uninhibited when intoxicated, and she is trying to stay faithful to her out-of-town boyfriend, she may avoid drinking alcohol so as not to put herself in a compromising situation.

In a clinical setting, learning the reasons for young-adult drinkers, drinking (especially if their drinking frequently leads to negative consequences) is critical in helping them change their drinking behavior. For example, if someone typically drinks to feel sociable, clinicians can work with the person to come up with ways to be social without alcohol (e.g., joining a club that meets in the evenings, going to the gym late at night to mingle with their peers). For clients who report that they typically drink to relax, clinicians can help them brainstorm other techniques for relaxation (e.g., going for a run, watching a movie with roommates). In summary, knowing a client's motivation to drink can help clinicians focus on what it is that the client is trying to get from alcohol, and generate alternatives to drinking or risky drinking that have the potential to achieve a similar outcome. One of the most commonly used drinking motives measures is the previously mentioned DMQ-R (Cooper, 1994), which has been psychometrically evaluated for use in undergraduate college students by Grant et al. (2007). The DMQ-R is a 20-item measure with 5-point rating scales, and includes items such as *I drink because it's exciting* and *I drink to forget my worries*. As discussed earlier in the chapter "Theories and Models of Alcohol Misuse" (see Chapter 2), the DMQ-R yields four primary scales or types of motivation (i.e., social motives, coping motives, enhancement motives, social conformity motives).

3.6 Readiness to Change

Assessing clients' readiness to change their alcohol use at the beginning of treatment can be very helpful for understanding where they are (e.g., not ready to change, ambivalent or undecided, ready to change) and how to initially interact with them (Miller & Rollnick, 2012). For example, knowing that a young-adult binge drinker is not ready for, or sees no need to, change despite repeated negative consequences, tells a clinician to use reflection to get such individuals to give voice to the change process or what it might take to change (see Section 4.2.4 "Intervention Style," on motivational interviewing for ways to do this). As will also be discussed in this section, the treatment approach with this client would be to start very slow, possibly by just discussing the good and "not as good" features of the client's recent drinking experiences to get them to think about what they "*get out of*" drinking.

A simple and quick way to evaluate readiness to change is to use a *readiness ruler,* a scaling strategy that conceptualizes readiness or motivation to change along a continuum (Heather, Smailes, & Cassidy, 2008). This tool uses a visual analogue of a ruler (see Figure 2). Clients are asked to use the ruler to give voice to how ready they are to change at the *present time* (a state measure) on a 10-point scale, where 1 = *definitely not ready to change* and 10 = *definitely ready to change*. A readiness ruler allows clinicians to immediately know their clients' level of motivation or readiness for change. Depending on this level, a conversation can develop between the client and clinician using different motivational strategies and techniques. For example, with unmotivated or not ready clients who choose a low number (e.g., 1–4), clinicians can ask, "*What would have to happen for you to go from a 3 to a 5?*" The readiness ruler can also help clients give voice to how they have changed, what they need to do to change further, and how they feel about changing. To highlight

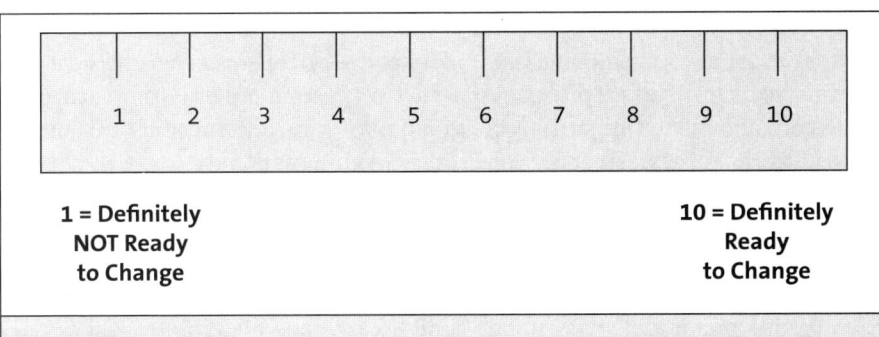

Figure 2
Example of a readiness ruler to be used at the beginning of treatment. Clinicians can modify rulers as they see fit.

any readiness on the part of clients, clinicians can prompt them to voice their reasons for change by asking why they are at a certain, relatively higher number (e.g., "Why would you say you're at a 7 instead of a 5 or 6?"). Once the client selects a number on the ruler, follow-up questions like those shown above allow clinicians to get a detailed picture of where clients are on the change continuum, while also providing clients with an opportunity to discuss their current situation and thoughts about drinking. It should be noted that there are many existing formats for readiness rulers, with varying numbers of written statements along the line. Many clinicians use rulers with different anchor points and numbers.

3.7 Influential Factors for Treatment

Clinicians entering into treatment with a young-adult client have many things to consider. For example, are there co-occurring conditions that require a different or simultaneous treatment? Incorporating information about the client's prior treatment experiences, should a new or similar approach be tried? The following sections discuss some factors to consider when making such decisions. Suggestions about what clinical tools and measures might be useful during the early stages of treatment are provided.

3.7.1 Current and Past Mental and Physical Health Problems

To get a full picture of clients' presenting concerns, clinicians should assess for physical and mental health problems (unrelated to alcohol) before deciding on a course of treatment. For example, the presence of some major medical conditions (e.g., diabetes, ulcers, possible pregnancy) might restrict the types of medications patients could take and influence whether or not it is potentially dangerous for them to consume alcohol, even in moderate amounts. In addition, many young problem drinkers also have co-occurring psychiatric diagnoses (e.g., depression, attention deficit or eating disorders), and a semistructured or structured diagnostic interview will provide clinicians with a good understanding of the client's areas of concern besides alcohol use.

It is important for clinicians to understand a client's relevant medical and psychiatric history before proceeding with treatment in order to prioritize areas of concern and make sure all aspects of pathology are addressed. For example, some diagnostic assessments (e.g., the Mini-International Neuropsychiatric Interview [MINI]) allow for the scorer to indicate which disorder is the "primary diagnosis," as well as which "meet criteria." In the event that a disorder other than an AUD is deemed the "primary diagnosis" (according to the clinician's judgment, based on the severity of the respective problems), that primary disorder should be part of the initial treatment evaluation, with the AUD captured under the primary disorder, but not as the main focus for treatment. For example, for young-adult clients who meet criteria for generalized anxiety disorder (GAD), and report drinking as a way of coping with frequent anxiety, clinicians could begin cognitive behavioral therapy (CBT) for anxiety (i.e., targeting certain negative cognitions and then the behavioral responses) as the primary treatment modality. Within this treatment context, alcohol misuse and binge drinking will certainly get addressed as one of the ways in which the client is handling his or her anxiety in a maladaptive way, and other, more adaptive coping strategies will be generated through client–clinician discussion and strategizing (e.g., breathing exercises). This approach targets the GAD symptoms as the primary concern, together with the alcohol use resulting from those symptoms.

For clients whose self-reports and assessments do not reveal any problem areas other than alcohol use, the clinician should feel confident identifying drinking as the primary treatment focus and using one of the evidence-based treatment approaches described in the sections on methods of treatment (see Chapter 4).

3.7.2 Treatment History

As with all clients who use alcohol, it is important to ask young people if they have ever been in any kind of alcohol treatment or self-help group, and getting them to comment on whether the treatment was helpful or not can be used to better inform the current treatment plan.

> **Clinical Pearl**
> **Talking About Treatment History**
>
> How the client talks about past treatment experiences may also be related to his/her readiness to change. For example, pay attention to how much the clients place external blame – such as faulting therapists, rehab facilities, or specific policies for their lack of treatment "success." If clients make little or no mention of ways in which they could have gotten (or still can get) more out of treatment, this might reflect lack of ownership of the problem and be a sign that they have low levels of readiness to change.

Clients who did not find treatment helpful can be asked what would need to be different for them to change their alcohol use. For some clients, prior treatment approaches may have felt completely alien or unacceptable, while other clients might report that they learned a great deal from previous experiences, and just were not "in the right place" to make changes at that time. Some clients might have found their last treatment experience to be very helpful, but their drinking has continued to be problematic for other reasons, or problematic drinking has recurred after a period of abstinence or nonproblem drinking. Such probing provides a good opportunity for clients and clinicians to collaborate about what might be effective in helping them change their alcohol use. Because AUDs are sometimes refractory and can require multiple quit attempts, clinicians should refrain from giving clients the impression that their past attempts were failures.

3.7.3 Identifying the Appropriate Treatment

Once clinicians feel satisfied that their client's problem drinking is adequately assessed and they understand the client's level of consumption, scope and severity of consequences, and readiness to change, they can decide on the best course of treatment. Treatment should be evidence-based and empirically supported, as well as consistent with a client's value system, priorities, and the clinician's area and level of experience. Evidence-based treatments that have been shown to work with young adults should be considered over non-evidence-based treatments no matter how appealing the latter appear to be. The major evidence-based interventions for young-adult heavy and problem drinkers can be categorized into a handful of approaches, many of which overlap (i.e., harm reduction, CBT, self-change, personalized feedback, brief interventions [BIs], and motivational interviewing). Each of these approaches will be described in detail in the sections on methods of treatment (see Chapter 4).

Many factors should be considered before planning a course of treatment, particularly the severity of a client's drinking problem and treatment history, with more severe and/or treatment-resistant drinkers requiring more intensive treatments than less severe, never-treated drinkers. In addition, as discussed in a following section (see Section 4.2.3), a stepped-care or "treatment tiering" approach, based on patient information and clinical judgment, should be considered. A stepped-care approach suggests starting with the most minimally invasive, least costly, and least time-consuming treatment that has both good outcomes and high consumer satisfaction. If not successful, treatment can then be "stepped up" to a more intense or different treatment (Sobell & Sobell, 2000). This model encompasses many different treatment approaches, and is designed to accommodate individual differences.

4 Treatment

4.1 Methods of Treatment

4.1.1 Evidence-Based and Empirically Supported Treatment

Practitioners working with young-adult drinkers can avail themselves of several different empirically supported treatment approaches and interventions to help their clients change their alcohol use. In this section, we will review components of interventions as well as some integrated treatment programs that have been shown, through well controlled and designed studies, to significantly help young-adult problem drinkers stop drinking or reduce their drinking to nonrisky drinking levels.

4.1.2 Overview of Existing Treatment Components

The empirically supported treatment components discussed in this section are most often (and effectively) used in combination rather than as stand-alone methods. Some of the components are about specific treatment strategies or *things to do* (e.g., provide personalized feedback to the client), whereas others are more about *how to do it* (e.g., while expressing empathy or by creating discrepancies – both a part of a motivational enhancement style). Clinicians should note that these treatment components are intended to be used with young-adult binge and problem drinkers, who tend not to be severely dependent drinkers, and therefore the approaches described here may not always be well suited for chronic heavy drinkers who are older and/or display symptoms of severe dependence.

We begin with a general overview of the harm-reduction perspective, as this is a broad and versatile approach for viewing and addressing change in addictive behaviors and sets the stage for the discussion of specific strategies and therapeutic styles. We then present a discussion of treatment content (i.e., what to do), specifically a review of several CBT techniques and personalized feedback. Next we discuss treatment formats (i.e., how to do it), with a focus on screening and BI and how to step up the care of individuals who need more help. We then consider how a motivational approach and style (i.e., motivational interviewing) can be used to help young drinkers increase their motivation to consider changing their alcohol use. A few specific formal treatment strategies that integrate these components will then be discussed, including some emerging interventions. Finally, we will discuss the course of young-adult alcohol misuse, multicultural issues in treatment, and potential problems that clinicians might encounter when working with young-adult problem drinkers.

4.2 Mechanisms of Action and Efficacy of Individual Approaches

When applicable, we will include brief sections on the mechanisms of action and the efficacies of various treatment components discussed in this chapter. Mechanisms of action refer to the specific aspects of a treatment that are responsible for the therapeutic effect. Nearly all face-to-face approaches for treating alcohol misuse involve discussion and social interaction to increase skill use, enhance motivation, and modify cognitions to reduce the negative effects of risky or problem drinking. Although the specific means by which interventions work are difficult to define precisely, especially when the programs are multimodal, researchers have attempted to identify specific mechanisms of action for some of the widely used strategies for decreasing alcohol misuse among young adults. For clinicians, knowing this information can be useful when outlining the course of treatment for a young-adult problem drinker. For example, if a provider's time is limited, it may help to know which aspects of a certain treatment are the most "important" (i.e., shown to be most responsible for behavior change), and those that might not be as necessary. Even when time and resources are not an issue, understanding the mechanisms of change can help providers better understand which treatment tools to implement.

Regarding treatment efficacy (i.e., ability of a treatment to produce a desired or intended result), numerous studies have been conducted on many of the components discussed in this chapter. Because different treatment components are often implemented together, efficacy studies are rarely able to focus on stand-alone treatment aspects or components. Rather, they focus on methods that use elements of a treatment approach, compared with methods that do not, or compared with no-treatment control groups. When applicable, existing evidence of the efficacy of certain treatment components will be reviewed following the initial discussion of the component, in an effort to help clinicians be better informed when deciding on a course of treatment for their clients.

4.2.1 Intervention Approach

Harm Reduction
Young-adult problem drinkers are more likely to be open to harm-reduction strategies than to traditional approaches that require an abstinence-only goal. Harm-reduction approaches posit that alcohol misuse, abuse, and dependence can be placed on a continuum of harmful consequences, and the goal of treatment should be movement along that continuum from more to less (and fewer) harmful effects. Although abstinence is often considered the "anchor point" of minimal consequences, any reduction in substance-related problems (i.e.,

movement along the continuum in the direction of abstinence) is actively encouraged. For example, an intervention that results in clients stopping what may have been a frequent habit of driving drunk, and instead consistently finding alternative means of safe transportation, would be considered a "success" within a harm-reduction framework, even if the client did not actually reduce or stop drinking.

For young-adult drinkers, intervention approaches with a harm-reduction perspective (Marlatt & Witkiewitz, 2002) have been successful for several reasons. First, we know that many problem drinkers report that they have avoided entering treatment because of the stigma associated with the disease model of alcoholism (Klingemann & Sobell, 2007) and the requirement of total abstinence as the only treatment goal (for a review of this model, see White, 2000). Indeed, for young adults, a lifetime commitment to complete abstinence may be intimidating or overwhelming to contemplate, resulting in an avoidance of treatment altogether. Therefore, clinicians amenable to entertaining or encouraging goals other than abstinence might be able to engage some avoidant clients and/or keep clients in treatment who would otherwise leave. Interventions that allow for the possibility of future drinking, but focus on reducing the harm often associated with intoxication, may be more appealing and "doable" for young adults, and thus increase their likelihood of seeking (and staying in) treatment. Programs that follow a harm-reduction model – for example, the School Health and Alcohol Harm Reduction Project (SHARP; McBride, Midford, Farringdon, & Phillips, 2000) and Brief Alcohol Screening and Intervention for College Students (BASICS; Dimeff, Baer, Kivlahan, & Marlatt, 1999) – have been found to be efficacious in the reduction of alcohol-related harm ranging from missed school or work to interpersonal conflict resulting from alcohol consumption. In addition to the focus on outcomes not restricted to abstinence, one aspect of harm-reduction approaches that appeals to young adults (and, likely, adolescents and older adults), is the emphasis on a nonjudgmental stance and supportive nature of the provider. Because harm-reduction interventions view addictive behaviors as a health issue rather than a punishable offense or moral transgression, the dialogue that takes place between clients and practitioners takes the form of a motivational interview, eliciting (i.e., evoking or prompting) collaborative conversation about behaviors and events, rather than a one-sided lecture. In a supportive atmosphere, young adults may be more likely to be engaged and receptive to feedback than they will be in an environment where they are made to feel that they have done something of which they should be ashamed and must completely avoid in the future.

Harm-reduction approaches do not all adhere to the same format, length, or modality, but interventions designed within the harm-reduction framework all share a common focus on the reduction of negative consequences rather than the mere reduction of drinking. Though some may argue that the simple discussion of illegal behaviors (such as underage drinking) at schools and in young-adult settings leads to an increase in use because the behavior seems to be condoned, this concern appears to be unfounded. Clinicians treating young adults should be encouraged to provide pragmatic feedback about how to "drink safely" should one choose to consume alcohol. All of the treatment approaches and strategies covered in this chapter could safely be described as

Harm-reduction approaches are characterized by the supportive and nonjudgmental nature of the practitioner

Young adults may be particularly averse to the idea of a permanent future of abstinence

falling under a harm-reduction model, in that they aim to work with clients to achieve the best possible outcomes, whether that be abstinence, reducing consumption, or adopting behavioral strategies to minimize the consequences of consumption. However, for clinicians, having clients who experience severe alcohol problems but do not want to quit drinking entirely can sometimes lead to a dilemma in terms of ethics, liability, and deciding on the best way to proceed with treatment. For example, is it worth working with very dependent drinkers on strategies for moderate consumption, even though they may have tried that before and "failed," and their problems have since become worse? Unfortunately, because each clinical presentation is unique, there are no clear answers to this type of question. However, it is often advisable for clinicians to use a stepped-care treatment model, in which they start with the least invasive or demanding type of treatment (in this case, that might be one that does not require a goal of abstinence) and work up from there if initial approaches prove unsuccessful.

4.2.2 Intervention Content

Cognitive Behavioral Therapy and Self-Change

Cognitive behavioral and self-change strategies have been widely employed to combat young-adult heavy drinking. The essence of CBT techniques for behavior change can be described as having two core components: (a) identifying behavior(s) to change, and (b) understanding the functional relationship between an individual's behavior and the context in which those behaviors are displayed. For young-adult drinkers, the behavior in question may not be alcohol consumption itself, but rather a potentially hazardous consequence of drinking that only occurs when they are intoxicated (e.g., drunk driving, risky sex, blackouts). The clinician should use the client's responses and the resulting discussion from the assessment of alcohol consumption and consequences to help the client identify which alcohol-related issues to prioritize. In this way, cognitive behavioral alcohol interventions are often described as falling into the harm-reduction model, in that they do not require the client to have a goal of abstinence, but rather one of healthy, nonhazardous drinking behavior (although, if this can only be accomplished through abstinence, then abstinence may indeed be the goal). Cognitive behavioral interventions teach clients how to anticipate and manage specific high-risk trigger situations (i.e., time or place where an individual's sense of control is threatened, like getting a bad grade on a big exam, or being at a crowded keg party late at night). They also help clients work to increase balance and incorporate overall healthy lifestyle habits to reduce levels of vulnerability in general and thus be better prepared to successfully handle high-risk situations when they arise. This approach often teaches specific skills or provides tools and tactics for individuals to utilize when they are tempted to engage in risky behaviors.

> **CBT strategies aim to identify behaviors that may need to be changed and help clients understand how and why those behaviors come to be displayed**

> **A primary CBT strategy for problematic drinking focuses on teaching clients how to anticipate and manage particularly high-risk situations**

Researchers have identified many ways to use CBT when applied to alcohol use in young adults. These procedures can be used alone or in combination (see Table 6).

Table 6
Important Components of CBT for Alcohol Misuse

Component	Example of how it is implemented
Provide accurate information about alcohol	Provide info sheets with info about alcohol's health effects, how to calculate BAC, size of standard drinks, etc.
Identify personal risk factors	Discuss family history of alcoholism and personal history of externalizing disorders (e.g., ADHD) or behaviors (e.g., DUI citations)
Challenge myths and positive alcohol-related expectancies	Discuss what clients "*think*" happens as a result of drinking and how often this is actually the case for them
Establish appropriate and safe-drinking goals	Have clients come up with *their own* realistic goals and why they set them (e.g., limiting number of drinks to four to avoid blacking out)
Identifying, managing, and learning from high-risk situations	Conduct a functional analysis about the last problematic drinking episode to help clients understand the identifiable antecedents of certain situations and the possible consequences so they can be prepared in the future
Attain lifestyle balance	Discuss substance-free activities that clients enjoy and how they could realistically incorporate them more often
Increase feelings of self-efficacy	Point out clients' recent instances of success (e.g., when they turned down a drink) and ask them to explain how they were able to do it
Self-monitoring techniques	Provide clients with blank daily drinking logs to monitor their daily risk factors, alcohol consumption, and associated consequences

Note. ADHD = attention deficit/hyperactivity disorder; BAC = blood alcohol concentration; CBT = cognitive behavioral therapy; DUI = driving under the influence.

Provide Accurate Information About Alcohol

A very common element of alcohol interventions for young adults is the provision of information (often in the form of *personalized feedback*), which can be presented in different formats. For example, young-adult drinkers can be presented with details about the short- and long-term effects of risky alcohol consumption, instructions on how to calculate one's BAC, the size of standard drinks, normative drinking patterns of others in their age and demographic group, specifics about alcohol metabolism, and even the caloric content of certain alcoholic beverages. To provide accurate information to clients, clinicians can search the Web for accurate information or use some of the many publicly available online resources designed to give personalized feedback to problem drinkers (see the section "Personalized Feedback," below).

Identify Personal Risk Factors

Identifying personal risk factors is an aspect of CBT interventions that focuses on aspects of drinkers' histories that may place them at greater risk for engaging in alcohol misuse. For example, those with a positive family history of AUDs (O'Neill, Parra, & Sher, 2001) or a history of externalizing disorders (e.g., conduct disorder; Kessler et al., 1997) are, in general, at heightened risk for engaging in harmful behaviors when under the influence. Individuals high in traits such as anxiety sensitivity, novelty seeking, sensation seeking, and overall impulsivity are more likely to be heavy drinkers and experience alcohol-related problems. In addition to clarifying these general risk factors, clinicians should also speak with clients about individual factors such as certain types of emotional response patterns or particular "triggers" for risky use.

Challenge Myths and Positive Alcohol-Related Expectancies

Another aspect of a CBT approach includes examining and challenging existing positive beliefs about alcohol and its effects (for example, "more is better"). Such challenging would include the presentation of information about alcohol's placebo effects, to help clients understand which aspects of the drinking environment are due to actual pharmacological properties of alcohol, and which are not.

Establish Appropriate and Nonrisky Drinking Goals

An important first step in making changes involves having clear goals and a treatment plan. Because establishing drinking goals is not something most clients do or think about prior to entering treatment, it is important to make this part of the treatment plan from the beginning of treatment. Goal setting in CBT is often less educational and more action-oriented. To develop appropriate drinking-related treatment goals, clinicians should ask clients several key questions with respect to how they view their drinking behavior currently, how they envision possible future drinking behavior, and their confidence in achieving a low-risk drinking goal (see Sobell & Sobell, 2011, pp. 51–53). Some CBT interventions systematically explore goal choice with all clients by having them complete a homework exercise called "Goal Choice Evaluation for Alcohol Use" (Sobell & Sobell, 2011, pp. 75–77). This exercise asks clients to identify the nature of their current goal (either "not to drink at all" or "to drink only in certain ways"), and contains specific items for clients to rate the importance of their goal (e.g., *"Is my goal important enough that I will work to achieve it even if progress is slow or difficult?"*). Clinicians should remind clients that they can change their goal over time and resist the urge to impose their own clinical opinions on what the clients' goals *should* be. Lastly, it is important for clinicians to be aware that some clients may have specific social (e.g., a court order) or medical (e.g., a serious health condition) reasons for which any consumption of alcohol is contraindicated. In these instances, the clinician may need to more direct and spend time discussing reason(s) the client should abstain from alcohol. In the end, clients will still act on their own accord, but when alcohol is clearly contraindicated, it may become a liability issue when therapists encourage moderation rather than abstinence. Additionally, clinicians who have a discussion of this nature with a client are advised to document it in the clinical record. (For a discussion of specific contraindications to low-risk drinking and whether moderate drinking is a good fit for young drinkers, see Sobell & Sobell, 2011, p. 83.)

Although it is tempting for clinicians to give advice or make suggestions as to why a client's drinking is contraindicated (e.g., legal or social sanctions), it is counterproductive to be argumentative or insistent. For young-adult clients, this type of approach typically comes across as paternalistic and disrespectful, and it will more likely result in defensiveness than concession. Instead, clinicians should engage in a conversation with clients using a motivational interviewing style to have the clients give voice to what might happen if they continue drinking or why others think low-risk drinking is not a good fit for them at the present time. In some of these instances, a harm-reduction approach may be the best way to proceed if the client resists being abstinent. When people establish their own treatment goals, it engenders feelings of autonomy and ownership about the course and outcomes of treatment, underscoring the importance of clients coming up with their own goals and objectives at the onset of treatment in order to maintain motivation and attain the best possible treatment outcomes (e.g., Booth, Dale, Slade, & Dewey, 1992). If clients are unable to achieve a low-risk drinking goal, this often becomes apparent to them, and many such clients decide for themselves that abstinence is the best course (e.g., Saladin & Santa Ana, 2004).

Moderate drinking (defined as ≤ 4 drinks on any single day and ≤ 14 drinks per week for men and ≤ 3 drinks on any single day and ≤ 7 drinks per week for women; National Institute on Alcohol Abuse and Alcoholism, 2014) is associated with low levels of health risks (compared with heavy drinking). Because of the implicit appeal of moderate drinking when juxtaposed to abstinence, clinicians have ample reason to support a client's goals of drinking reduction (and other harm-reduction alternatives) during the goal-setting portion of treatment. The NIAAA has produced a freely downloadable 16-page evidenced-based pamphlet, *Rethinking Drinking*, in Spanish and English, which provides valuable, research-based information and drinking guidelines, and allows drinkers to take a look at their drinking habits and how they may affect their health (NIAAA, 2007b).

Identify, Manage, and Learn From High-Risk Situations

Learning how to recognize, handle, and rebound from high-risk situations are key aspects of CBT relapse prevention interventions for young-adult alcohol misuse (Marlatt & Witkiewitz, 2002). Both identification and management of risky situations are logically connected to one another because if drinkers cannot identify such a situation then they will not be able to "manage" it. Inevitably, however, many clients will encounter risky situations, and many will have setbacks, slips, or relapses. Such occasions can provide valuable learning experiences for clients, and, if they arise, should be discussed thoroughly and nonjudgmentally during the course of the treatment.

Identifying High-Risk Situations

Evidence-based treatment programs work to increase clients' awareness of their own hazardous drinking behavior. Learning to identify high-risk situations includes self-monitoring (e.g., keeping track of where, why, and how many drinks are consumed) and in-session discussion of situational and contextual factors that increase one's desire to drink heavily (e.g., reuniting with old friends; going out after a week of intense studying; lighting up a cigarette). In addition, the BSCQ (Breslin et al., 2000) can be used to help gauge clients' abilities to resist drinking heavily in different situations. For example, clients are asked to indicate how confident they are at the present time (0% = *not at all confident*, 100% = *totally confident*) that they can resist the urge to drink heavily in situations involving unpleasant emotions (e.g., feeling depressed) or pleasant emotions (e.g., when feeling like celebrating). Reviewing a client's BSCQ responses during the session can help them increase their knowledge about what makes a situation "risky," and it helps young drinkers improve their ability to correctly identify those situations early on and thus be more prepared to manage them effectively.

Within a cognitive behavioral clinical context, identification of high-risk situations requires a thorough assessment of situations that could be particularly tempting for a given client. This type of assessment can be done informally through discussion, with the clinician probing about specific situations or environmental stressors that have come up recently or might come up in the future. For example, the clinician could start the conversation by asking, *"Can you tell me about the types of situations that make you feel very tempted to drink to excess?"* and then, with the participation of the client, breaking down aspects of those situations in terms of the social, emotional, and contextual factors that may or may not typically be present. The clinician should be prepared for answers that vary in specificity. Some clients might respond with something that sounds very general (e.g., *"When it's nice outside"*), whereas others might give more detailed responses (e.g., *"When I visit my family and my mother says something that makes me mad"*). In either instance, clinicians should follow-up and ask clients to try to identify what feelings are often associated with those situations that might make them feel tempted to drink. Is it excitement? Anxiety? Boredom?

Managing High-Risk Situations

For problem drinkers (and those at risk of developing problem behaviors), managing high-risk situations related to drinking includes further discussion of the antecedents and precipitating factors and emotions. Once consistent triggers are identified (e.g., getting into a fight with a boyfriend or girlfriend, feeling particularly excitable, finishing a big exam and wanting to release tension), the client and therapist can discuss how to identify and manage when these situations might come up in the future and then spend in-session time discussing and role-playing how that situation would be handled in "real life." Though it may seem unusual or awkward to rehearse such scenarios with a 20-year-old, this provides a good opportunity for the client and therapist to identify strengths and weaknesses of the client's strategy, and fine-tune the approach in vivo. The following tactics may be helpful: Have clients remind themselves of their drinking goal and limits; use imagery (e.g., picturing themselves waking up in the morning feeling healthy and not hungover); and use behavioral strategies to reduce the rate of drinking (e.g., spacing drinks out longer, alternating alcoholic beverages with nonalcoholic beverages, or leaving the situation to go somewhere without alcohol – e.g., to an arcade or campus-sponsored event).

More broadly, there should also be a focus on implementing general self-change and lifestyle strategies to help with goal maintenance during and after treatment (see section below "Attaining Lifestyle Balance"). This part of the therapy focuses on reducing daily stress and increasing pleasurable events in the clients' lives to decrease general levels of vulnerability and, in turn, make them more equipped to handle negative emotions or particularly strong urges to drink. A motivational approach recommends that clinicians try to make most discussions with clients a collaborative dialogue rather than a lecture, by using reflections and having clients give voice to the change process.

Learning From Slips

Slips, lapses, and *goal violations* are a normal and predictable part of almost all behavior change processes, including changing drinking behavior. Cognitive behavioral interventions incorporate slips or lapses as part of relapse prevention interventions, and CBT clinicians frame slips as learning opportunities rather than failures. With this perspective, when slips occur, clients and therapists can learn what triggered the lapse and develop a better plan to deal with such events in the future. Essentially what is occurring is a functional behavioral analysis of the event to increase clients' awareness of the antecedents and consequences of the slip or lapse. During the behavioral analysis, a clinician could address the antecedents of the event (having a fight with a friend, for example) by asking the client to discuss what was happening prior to the drinking episode (e.g., Had anything happened that was particularly troubling or particularly exciting? What were the client's hopes and expectations for how the night would turn out?). Such discussions can also address the client's emotional and cognitive states leading up to and during the drinking episode, as well as at which points different coping skills could have been used or different decisions could have been made. For example, the client may reveal that he or she was really looking forward to going out with a group of friends and, prior to even heading to the bars, had already consumed three drinks while prepartying. Using a motivational style, the clinician could say to the client, *"Help me understand how drinking this much early in the night would help you stick to your 4-drink limit."* Such a query would allow the client to give voice to the fact that it would not, and thus avoid the clinician lecturing the client. Then the clinician could respond to the client by saying, *"What do you think you could do next time a similar situation arises to avoid drinking this much?"*

Clinical Pearl
Setting Drinking Limits

It should be noted that four drinks for a woman is considered binge drinking, and drinking this much has been shown to be associated with certain health risks and various types of alcohol-related consequences. For this reason, the clinician might be hesitant to support such a limit, and feel tempted to convince the client to set a lower limit, perhaps of three drinks on a given occasion. Though this should be raised and it would be ideal if the client was willing and receptive, for many young drinkers who are used to a lifestyle of heavy binge drinking and late night partying, this might frankly be unrealistic for them, and the mere suggestion could result in them adamantly expressing their doubt and disfavor. Should this happen, the harm-reduction model would encourage clinicians to accept the

> client's self-made goal of four drinks, since it is less risky than the larger amount (of perhaps eight to 12) that she was accustomed to consuming. Recall that any movement along the continuum of more to less harm is considered progress in this model and should be encouraged.

A behavioral analysis can also reveal what factors led to continued overconsumption throughout the evening (e.g., Did people buy drinks that the client didn't want to refuse? Did an initial negative interaction with the client's friend prompt him or her to try to reduce their distress by drinking more?), as well as what, if anything, immediately triggered the fight with the friend. By discussing what led up to drinking excessively and fighting, the client can gain increased awareness about the contributing factors and identify ways in which he or she could have used different coping skills (e.g., going outside for fresh air instead of ordering another drink after the initial interaction with an unpleasant friend). What also needs to occur between the client and therapist is an open discussion about how the client felt about his or her goal violation. This approach helps clients identify instances in which they could have made more effective or goal-consistent choices, and is in contrast to the idea that failure to meet one's goal is a failure of the treatment more generally.

> **Clinical Pearl**
> **Marlatt's Relapse Prevention Model**
>
> The element of CBT interventions that treats goal violations as opportunities for learning and skill building rather than as failures is tied to Marlatt's relapse prevention model.

Marlatt's Relapse Prevention Model

The element of CBT interventions that treats goal violations as opportunities for learning and skill building rather than as failures is closely tied to Marlatt's relapse prevention model (RP model; Marlatt & Donovan, 2005), which emphasizes the importance of the maintenance phase of the behavior change process, rather than (or at least as much as) the initial change phase, and touts the potential benefits of lapses as occasions to implement new proactive and reactive intervention strategies. More specifically, Marlatt's RP model has two primary aims: (1) to prevent an initial lapse and maintain treatment goals of abstinence or harm reduction and (2) to provide *lapse management* if a lapse occurs, in order to prevent a future relapse (Marlatt & Donovan, 2005). Indeed, the cognitive behavioral model of relapse is centered on individuals' responses in high-risk situations, which are formed by the interaction between personal (affective, coping, self-efficacy) and environmental (social influences, access to alcohol) risk factors. For example, if drinkers have low confidence in their ability to handle situations effectively, they may be more likely to give in to temptation, especially if there are strong external cues present (such as being at a party with a fully stocked bar). Individuals who give in may also be influenced by the abstinence violation effect (AVE; discussed by Witkiewitz & Marlatt, 2004), which refers to the feelings of guilt, shame, and loss of control that an individual experiences following the violation of self-imposed rules. The cognitive component of the AVE assumes that if drinkers attribute their lapses to internal factors that are stable and uncontrollable, their risk for relapse will be even greater because these instances of weakness will appear indicative of a more global and permanent weakness that cannot be overcome. Clinicians working within the RP model are taught to discourage these negative and global attributions by highlighting the normalcy of lapses as well as the ways in which the client was masterful and successful during that same situation or others.

The RP model is educational and works to restructure existing cognitions in an effort to prevent a lapse, which is a return to an addictive or problematic behavior. Lapses should be considered a natural and inevitable part of the treatment process, and they can be used to help clients avoid a *major relapse,* which is a return to an addictive or problematic lifestyle which is likely to result in a series of harms and heightened risk levels. Indeed, clinicians focusing on relapse prevention are taught to communicate to clients that lapses should not be viewed as indications of poor willpower, but instead as a natural aspect of any attempt at behavior change and something that, if discussed and managed effectively, can equip individuals with the knowledge and tools to better adhere to their own goals in the future, even when confronted with a highly tempting situation.

Attaining Lifestyle Balance

A key aspect of CBT interventions for young-adult problem drinkers is encouraging a healthy, balanced lifestyle, with an improved sense of general well-being. During treatment this can be communicated through discussion of healthy, positive, non-substance-related activities that clients can enjoy (e.g., running, playing sports, volunteering). Clinicians need to avoid imposing their own ideas about reducing daily stress, and instead solicit ideas from clients (e.g., *"What kinds of things do you think might help you reduce your daily stress? What has worked for you before? What would you like to try this next time?"*).

For college students in particular, clinicians should also go over the person's study, work, and party patterns, paying careful attention to ways in which patterns might lead to greater distress and urges to engage in risky excessive drinking. For example, it is quite common for students to cram for exams and study very intensely for short periods of time at the end of the semester, and then feel they can "reward" themselves and "let loose" with binge drinking episodes. Clinicians might talk to such clients about how feasible it would be to work and study steadily throughout the semester to be better able to incorporate rest and fun when academic "crunch time" arrives. Clinicians could also ask clients if they did not pull an all-nighter and cram for exams, how they would feel differently at the end of the semester.

Increase Self-Efficacy

Self-efficacy is an individual's belief that he or she can execute the skills needed to control a situation and achieve a desired outcome (Bandura, 2006). This construct has been widely studied in the area of addictive behavior due to the association between one's feelings of self-efficacy and related motivation and effort, and researchers have found that individuals' efficacy to manage high-risk situations is protective against relapse. In the context of an intervention, clinicians may be able to enhance clients' confidence and feelings of mastery by highlighting past success experiences (i.e., playing to a client's strengths; e.g., *"I remembered you said you quit smoking a few years ago. How might you use this experience in thinking about how to change your drinking?"*).

Self-Monitoring Techniques

Drinking self-monitoring involves recording one's drinking, usually on a daily basis. Self-monitoring, a well-established behavioral technique (Nelson & Hayes, 1981), is based on the principle that increased planning and self-awareness regarding alcohol misuse leads to less risky drinking and fewer negative consequences than would have been present without self-monitoring. Study results suggest that completing a diary anticipating alcohol consumption and problems, or even just keeping a log of one's own drinking, leads to fewer reported alcohol-related problems in college students. When starting an alcohol treatment program, therapists can encourage clients to self-monitor their alcohol use so it can be discussed in subsequent sessions. Though there are no standard forms of drinking logs, there are plenty of good templates available online for public use (see http://www.nova.edu/gsc/forms/client_handout_3_2_self-monitoring_logs_for_alcohol_use.pdf for printable versions, or see Appendix 2), or clients can make their own. At a minimum, the log should include the date, day of the week, documentation of any urges to drink, total number of drinks consumed per day, and whether or not that day's drinking led to problems. Preferably, more information about the timing and strength of each drink and the context of consumption would be obtained.

If clients appear resistant to maintaining logs, clinicians can try to point out the benefits of self-monitoring without coming across as demanding or controlling. Some points to include are the following: There are no "right" or "wrong" amounts to drink; the important thing is to be truthful; clients should give self-monitoring a chance before deciding if they do or do not like it; and bringing the drinking logs to each session helps clients and therapists work together to bring about change most effectively (more information on monitoring alcohol use is available at http://www.nova.edu/gsc/forms/Alcohol_SelfMonitor.pdf).

Mechanisms of Action in CBT Approaches

Cognitive behavioral treatment approaches to problematic drinking build on a primary principle: Excessive drinking and alcohol misuse often results in response to a deficit in effective coping strategies, so working to increase recognition of potentially problematic situations, as well as one's knowledge of cognitive and behavioral coping skills, helps individuals respond more adaptively to stressful cues. Though the exact elements of CBT that make it effective remain unknown (Morgenstern & Longabaugh, 2000), there are key components of the therapy that therapists should focus on when they conduct this treatment. Specifically, the functional analysis of drinking behavior is a crucial part of CBT for alcohol misuse because it helps clients better recognize the antecedents and consequences of their problematic drinking behavior. Antecedents can be environmental (e.g., it's one of the first warm days of summer), behavioral or interpersonal (e.g., a client just had a fight with a friend), or cognitive/emotional (e.g., a client feels particularly stressed out), and it is important for young-adult drinkers to know the difference if they are to be able to identify and respond effectively (i.e., without binge drinking) to these antecedents in the future. Once they have mastered the ability to understand their binge drinking triggers, and what often results from them, clients in CBT can learn to manage these situations themselves using problem solving, coping skills, and cognitive restructuring strategies when they find themselves faced with places, events, or feelings that they know are high risk.

Efficacy of CBT

Because the treatment approaches and components discussed in this chapter are most commonly and effectively used in combination rather than as stand-alone methods, specific studies of CBT used alone as a standardized approach to reduce young-adult drinking are rare. However, researchers have conducted evaluations of many of the components that are common in CBT interventions (skill building, alcohol expectancy challenge, goal setting, etc.) and tested their relative efficacy compared with one another. In an extensive review of 62 studies of college student drinking interventions, Carey and colleagues (Carey, Scott-Sheldon, Carey, & DeMartini, 2007) found that, at short-term follow-ups, interventions that had skills training or expectancy challenge components were less effective at reducing alcohol-related problem than interventions that utilized motivational interviewing, provided feedback about expectancies, motives, and/or normative comparisons, and included a decisional balance exercise. However, the authors were quick to note that the studies using skill training and expectancy challenge components had samples with higher proportions of high-risk and heavy drinkers, and that these preintervention characteristics were potentially responsible for the ostensibly smaller intervention effects.

Personalized Feedback

Providing personalized feedback about a drinker's alcohol consumption patterns (among other things) is routinely used in CBT interventions as a strategy for reducing alcohol use and alcohol-related problems among college students and young adults. Feedback can take many forms (see the section "Brief Computer-Based and Mobile Programs" for a further discussion of these options; e.g., *personal drinking profiles* such as drinking amounts and patterns, peak heavy and light BACs, money and calories spent on drinking; and *normative comparisons* such as the clients' beliefs about peers' drinking, amount they consume compared with relevant peer groups; Sobell & Sobell, 2011; Walters & Neighbors, 2005). There are several reasons that personalized feedback is an important part of CBT interventions with problem drinkers, particularly those who are younger (Miller & Rollnick, 2012; Sobell & Sobell, 2011): (a) it gives them information so they are more aware of their drinking behavior; (b) it gives them information which they can use to make better-informed decisions, and (c) it catalyzes the change process (i.e., tips the scale in favor of change or reduces ambivalence about changing). Clinicians interested in providing personalized feedback have a range of options, which vary in breadth and time requirements (see Appendix 3 for example of feedback measures and profiles). A research-based option that is widely used in college settings is the e-CHECKUP TO GO (also referred to as E-Chug: http://www.echeckuptogo.com/usa/), which is a commercially available program with

Drinking feedback can be delivered in person, during a computerized assessment, or through e-mail or snail mail

regularly updated normative data based on students from college campuses. Over 600 universities and colleges across 49 States, Canada, Australia, and Ireland use this program as a clinical tool for counselors and health professionals, a part of judicial sanctions for alcohol infractions, or as one element of a broader campus alcohol awareness program. Though these are designed to be self-guided (i.e., no face-to-face time is necessary), feedback profiles can be reviewed with a treatment provider to help the client process the information. The basic e-CHECKUP alcohol intervention takes approximately 20–30 min to complete, with the option of including a "Personal Reflections" portion at the end for an additional 15–20 min. The feedback includes information about respondents' drinking patterns (and how their drinking compares with that of others with similar demographic characteristics at their college), specific health and personal consequences, unique personal and familial risk factors, and local options for community support and emergency services. If a clinic or individual clinician purchases an e-CHECKUP account, it can be used on multiple occasions to track client progress. However, this program was specifically designed for use with a college student population, and therefore clinicians should note that some of the questions, feedback, and normative comparisons may not be applicable to young adults who are nonstudents. (For more options for free and for-purchase Web-based personalized feedback materials, see Walters & Neighbors, 2005.)

Irrespective of the nature of the feedback or how it is presented, motivational interviewing (Miller & Rollnick, 2012) stresses that feedback needs to be presented in a motivational enhancing manner (i.e., nonjudgmental, nonconfrontational, and not stigmatizing). Additionally, clinicians should ask open-ended questions (e.g., *"How does your drinking fit in with your academic goals?"*), provide affirmations (e.g., *"It looks like you've already tried very hard to cut back on your drinking"*), and give information summaries (e.g., *"So what I've heard is ... Is that right?"*). This regular interpersonal interaction demonstrates to clients that clinicians are "on their team" and, rather than judging them for their drinking behavior, are committed to working together to process what can often be a surprising and defense-inducing experience of being presented with one's own heavy drinking statistics.

When providing personalized feedback face-to-face is not an option or when trying to reach large numbers of people at once, using computer and smartphone technology has been shown to be an effective alternative that allows drinkers to interpret the information on their own. Providing feedback in such a manner is cost-effective, dissemination is easier, availability is 24/7, confidentiality is less of a problem, and interactive technology-based approaches are often more appealing to young people.

Mechanisms of Action With Personalized Feedback

The provision of feedback (either generic, personalized, or both) is usually only one component of many within an alcohol-related intervention. Therefore, it can be particularly difficult to isolate the unique effects of the feedback component and investigate its effectiveness and mechanisms of action. At its most basic level, the core assumption of the mechanism of action in personalized feedback is that the feedback increases drinkers' awareness of their drinking patterns and alcohol's effect on their lives, and that this awareness, and the potential discrepancy between their provided drinking profile and their beliefs, leads to feelings of discomfort. This discomfort (resulting from the mismatch between the way clients view themselves and what their drinking data say about their behavior) will lead to an increase in motivation to reduce their problematic drinking. For example, a college student client might experience discomfort from the discrepancy that results from a desire to go out drinking four nights a week but also wanting to get straight *A*s, realizing that these two desires are incompatible.

Efficacy of Personalized Feedback

Delivering feedback via computer, mail, or in-person has been found to be helpful in reducing drinking, with the addition of group or individual counseling sessions sometimes accompanying the feedback, and sometimes not (i.e., feedback can be provided as a stand-alone intervention). In fact, research studies have found that the feedback component drives the effect of the intervention, such that adding a counseling session does not significantly contribute to the short-term impact of the feedback (Walters & Neighbors, 2005). Indeed, reviews of clinical research trials have found computerized and mailed personalized feedback interventions (PFIs) to be more effective than control conditions (which did not include this component) and as effective as in-person PFIs (Larimer & Cronce, 2007), although other findings have demonstrated in-person PFIs to be slightly more effective (White, Young Mun, Pugh, & Morgan, 2007). In general, researchers and clinicians agree that both computerized and in-person personalized feedback approaches are effective in reducing alcohol consumption and alcohol-related consequences for young-adult problem drinkers, and that PFIs are relatively cost-effective BIs that should be conducted in the early stages of a drinker's alcohol problems whenever possible.

4.2.3   Intervention Formats

Brief Intervention

An empirically supported and increasingly used format for alcohol interventions with young adults is BIs. This format refers to drinkers who have one or more meetings (ranging from 5 min to six full sessions) with a health or mental health care provider to address their alcohol consumption and negative consequences, rather than going into more intensive outpatient or inpatient programs. The advantages of BIs are their appeal to people with less severe drinking problems, their ability to be administered by a variety of providers in a wide range of clinical settings, and their low cost compared with intense treatment options. Brief interventions are most common in health care settings (e.g., primary care offices and hospitals) and are ideally implemented following a screening for alcohol consumption and related problems – often referred to in the context of the evidence-based practice of Screening, Brief Intervention, and Referral to Treatment (SBIRT) program. They are intended to serve as early interventions, and be delivered prior to, or soon after, the onset of alcohol-related problems. In contrast to psychotherapy and general counseling techniques, BIs are described as educational, instructive, and motivational

> **Brief interventions usually consist of no more than one or two sessions, but can extend to as many as six**

> **Brief interventions are designed to be educational, instructive, and motivational. They include practical advice, but are not therapy sessions**

– they are designed to provide skills and practical advice about drinking rather than an environment for "talk therapy" or process work. Research has shown that many individuals with drinking problems are able to change on their own without formal help or treatment (e.g., Blomqvist, 2002). As is discussed later, BIs have received extensive empirical support through well-designed studies (e.g., Borsari & Carey, 2000; Dimeff, Baer, Kivlahan, & Marlatt, 1999), making them promising options for binge drinking young adults.

A typical BI for problem drinking would begin with a screening tool (such as the 10-item AUDIT; Reinert & Allen, 2007) that assesses a person's typical drinking patterns and related consequences. If the screening indicates that the individual is using alcohol in a risky or hazardous manner, then a BI is recommended. The US Department of Health and Human Services and the American College of Surgeons Committee on Trauma have published an outline for the intervention component of the SBIRT process (http://www.samhsa.gov/prevention/sbirt/). The first part of the intervention consists of the provision of information or feedback about the individual's screening results, as well as other educational information (e.g., the link between alcohol consumption and injury/health risks, guidelines for low-risk drinking, and strategies for reducing drinking and associated consequences). During the feedback about screening results, the practitioner is encouraged to compare the individual's scores with the norms of the measure, as well as define what scores would constitute low-, moderate, and high-risk drinking behavior. The second aspect of the BI includes a brief discussion between clients and their providers about the formers' reaction to the feedback information and their views toward drinking. This aspect of the BI is intended to encourage and elicit drinkers' honest opinions about what may or may not be problematic about their alcohol use, and how they may want to change their behavior to reduce their risk in the future. This component of a BI is feedback, but the feedback is brief so the intervention remains under a certain time limit. The third component of the BI involves clear and respectful advice from the clinician about ways to reduce alcohol-related risk, and working with the client to come up with a realistic change plan. As is the case with motivational approaches, the goal of BIs is for drinkers to establish their own goals and to verbalize or give voice to the best methods of achieving those goals. In the context of a BI, advice from a provider is recommended but should be presented in a nonjudgmental motivational manner.

> **Components of a BI:** Assessment and feedback about results, information about healthy drinking levels, honest discussion about client's reaction to feedback

Efficacy of Brief Interventions

Although BIs are successful in reducing levels of alcohol consumption, they are not necessarily more effective than extended treatments (Moyer, Finney, Swearingen, & Vergun, 2002), and their efficacy may differ across groups and study methodologies. Specifically, studies have found that BIs are most effective when the receiving population is non-treatment seeking (i.e., less severe; Moyer, Finney, Swearingen, & Vergun, 2002), and when the BI condition is compared with a no-treatment control condition (as opposed to an active or empirically validated approach; Vasilaki, Hosier, & Cox, 2006). Additionally, the effects of BIs are largest at the earliest follow-up points, and tend to decay over time (Moyer, Finney, Swearingen, & Vergun, 2002). Moreover, very few studies have included follow-ups of longer than 1 year, so it is difficult to know the long-term effects of BIs on problematic alcohol use and harmful consequences. In sum, BIs appear to be just as effective as extended treatments for individuals with mild to moderate alcohol problems. Therefore, because of the time and cost-efficiency associated with this treatment format, we recommend that medical and mental health providers conduct 5- to 15-min interviews with patients and clients who have screening results that indicate they are risky drinkers, before referring them to more intense or long-term treatment options. However, longer follow-up should be considered given the uncertain durability of some of the changes associated with BI.

Stepped Care

One research-supported approach to treatment is stepped care (see Figure 3). Stepped care refers to the practice of beginning treatment efforts with those methods that are consumer friendly, effective, and the least intrusive and expensive, and stepping up the care if it is deemed necessary to achieve the desired goal. This approach is *treatment tiering,* and it relies on empirically based guidelines to determine which treatment people should start with, and which treatment they should progress to (and when), should the initial strategy not be successful (Sobell & Sobell, 2000). For young-adult heavy drinkers, this tactic is likely the most sensible, given that brief, cost-effective interventions are often effective in promoting behavior change, and can save scarce resources. From a stepped-care perspective, a brief or minimal intervention would be considered the first step for most individuals with alcohol problems. However, if an outcome is not positive, then the treatment can be stepped up (e.g., more of the same intervention or a more intensive treatment or two simultaneous treatments, such as medication to manage urges coupled with a CBT intervention). However, if the evidence suggests that a severely dependent young binge drinker initially needs more than a brief treatment, the therapist can recommend and document the need for a more intensive approach.

Stepped care differs from treatment-matching approaches in that the subsequent, more intensive treatments are "performance based" (Sobell & Sobell, 2000); they are selected based both on pretreatment and within-treatment characteristics, rather than just pretreatment variables, as is done with treatment matching. For example, how much someone drank prior to the intervention would be useful information for making treatment decisions according to both approaches, but within a stepped-care paradigm, clients' drinking information *during* the treatment process (such as how much they drank while seeking treatment), can also be used to inform the next phase of treatment.

Conceptually, a stepped-care treatment paradigm makes sense. It is both cost and time efficient in that it does not waste time putting mild to moderate problem drinkers through intensive treatments without first trying more minimal alternatives. However, in practice, stepped-care treatment plans may be difficult for clinicians to carry out successfully due to a number of factors, such as client feasibility and willingness, and provider connectivity. Additionally, environmental factors, such as transportation problems and occupational and familial responsibilities, as well as client preferences, such as aversions to traditional treatment programs (which often emphasize total abstinence) may also work to deter many individuals from continuing up the hierarchy of care.

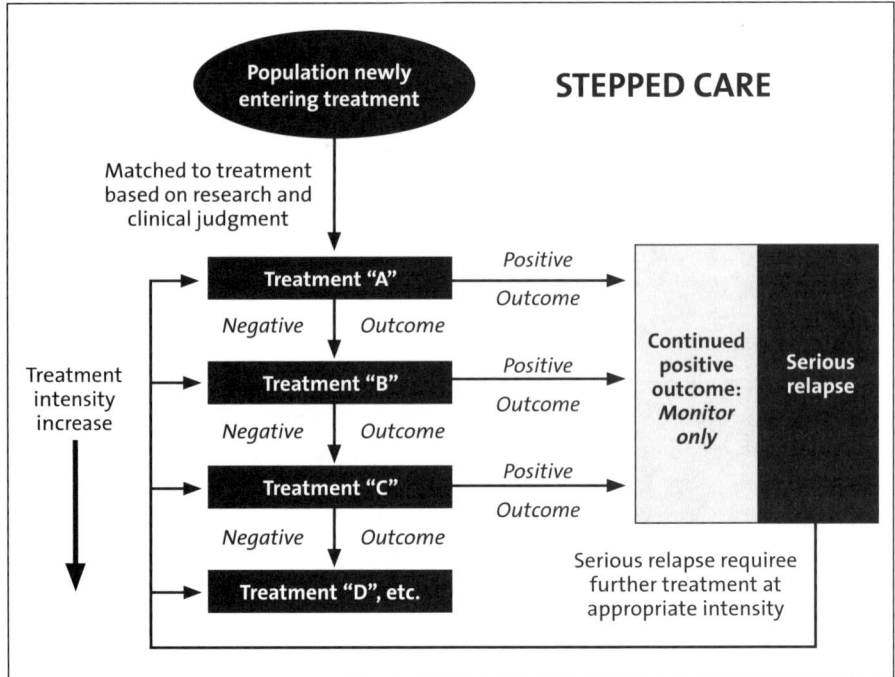

Figure 3
A stepped-care approach to the delivery of health care services.
Reprinted with permission from Baer, J. S., Marlatt, G. A., & McMahon, R. J. (Eds.). (1993). *Addictive behaviors across the lifespan: Prevention, treatment, and policy issues* (p. 150). Beverly Hills, CA: Sage. © 1993 by M. B. Sobell and L. C. Sobell.

4.2.4 Intervention Style

In addition to the content and the format of interventions for young-adult problem drinkers, the style and spirit of the intervention are of the upmost importance. Specifically, therapists and protocols that come across as controlling, judgmental, rigid, and demanding are likely to be met with client resistance, defensiveness, and lack of progress (Miller & Rollnick, 2012). In contrast, therapists who are eliciting, supportive of client autonomy, empathic, and warm are much more likely to see self-motivated behavior change in their clients.

The following section will discuss motivational interviewing (MI). Because adequate training in MI cannot be achieved just by reading this book section, interested clinicians are encouraged to visit the MI website (http://www.motivationalinterview.org) to obtain more resources and information about training opportunities. Readers are also encouraged to read the recent 3rd edition of Miller and Rollnick's seminal book for more ways to learn an MI approach (Miller & Rollnick, 2012).

Motivational Interviewing

MI is a set of communication skills (or a therapist's "way of being") designed to bring about behavior change by helping clients explore and resolve their own ambivalence about reducing their risky behavior(s) (see Table 7). Specifically, MI is a collaborative, client-centered, and directive approach. It is not an intervention in and of itself – rather, it is a set of techniques that can be applied to any of the intervention strategies discussed throughout this section. The style is collaborative and client-centered in that it is driven by the clients' input about their own lives and ideas for change, with therapist input also being encouraged. It is directive because therapists redirect or "steer" the conversation toward highlighting any discrepancy between clients' goals or values and their hazardous drinking behavior. It is through the increased awareness of discrepancies and the resolution of ambivalence about change that clients begin to think about implementing specific change strategies.

For many heavy drinking young adults, motivation to change can be low or there may be considerable ambivalence about the need to change. For example, they may frequently be surrounded by peers who drink as much as or more than they do. This can lead to drinkers thinking that their drinking is not "as bad" as their peers, and thus there is no need to change their habits. In this regard, it is important that interventions implementing an MI style focus on the *good things* and the *less good things* of drinking as they pertain to each drinker's own experiences.

Table 7
Important Strategies for Implementing a Motivational Interviewing Style

Strategy	How to
Express empathy	Give reflections (e.g., "It sounds like…" or "What I hear you saying is…")
Develop discrepancy	Highlight differences between client goals and current behavior
Avoid argumentation and roll with resistance	Do not challenge clients if they seem angry or defensive – instead, reflect (e.g., "It seems like this is tough for you to talk about right now…")
Support self-efficacy	Help clients improve their self-confidence. Note any positive changes they have made so far and have them explain how they did so
Assess readiness to change	Use a readiness ruler and meet clients "where they are at" in terms of motivation to change

Although use of MI does not require a specific protocol, its successful implementation relies on a continuous underlying focus on certain basic techniques that work to make sessions as productive as possible through increasing and maintaining motivation and readiness for change (Borsari & Carey, 2000). Although there are many clinical strategies that can help clients effectively resolve ambivalence and increase their motivation to change, the following MI strategies or techniques are most frequently used with clients: expressing empathy, developing discrepancy, rolling with resistance, and supporting self-efficacy.

Expressing Empathy
Empathy is one of the most critical aspects of a motivational approach. An empathic style (a) communicates respect for and acceptance of clients and

their feelings, (b) is characterized as a nonjudgmental, collaborative relationship between a therapist and a client, (c) establishes a safe and open environment for clients that allows them to be open and forthcoming with their therapists so that sensitive issues can be explored and examined, and (d) allows clients to make informed choices rather than have therapists tell them what to do. Empathy has been shown to be important in several studies that have demonstrated that high levels of empathy are associated with better outcomes for clients with SUDs (Moyers & Miller, 2013).

For therapists, being empathic essentially means communicating understanding. This is most often and effectively done through the use of reflective questions and statements during a session. Reflections can range in complexity, from simple repetition to rephrasing what the client said. Often, it involves making a small extension of clients' words, which allows them to clarify or elaborate as they see fit. For example, if clients talk about drinking being a very important part of their lives, a reasonable reflection might be *"It sounds like you have no interest in quitting drinking completely."* If the reflection is accurate, clients often feel they have been heard and respond with affirmations (e.g., *"Right, I would be fine to drink less but I'm definitely not going to stop drinking entirely"*), whereas if the reflection is "off base," they may respond with a correction (e.g., *"No, I do want to quit completely, I'm just saying it will be hard"*). Either way, reflections are useful for both therapists and clients – therapists are able to more accurately "zero in" on clients' true wishes and emotions, and clients are able to experience being actively listened to and understood.

Clinical Pearl
Reflective Listening

Generic examples of reflective listening
- "It sounds like…"
- "What I hear you saying…"
- "It seems like…"

Specific examples of reflective listening
- "It sounds like [insert experience of alcohol-related problem] was the first time you got concerned about your drinking…"
- "What I hear you saying is that you're afraid that cutting back on drinking will damage your social life…"

Adapted from Sobell & Sobell (2008).

Developing Discrepancy

Eliciting change talk can be used to address discrepancies between clients' words and actions (e.g., saying that they want to become abstinent, but continuing to engage in binge drinking) in a nonconfrontational, nonjudgmental manner (see Appendix 4 for examples of questions used to elicit change talk). When young-adult drinkers provide discrepant information, their therapists can use a motivational approach to point out or help them understand the discrepant information (e.g., *"On the one hand you reported getting two drunk driving arrests over the last 18 months, and yet on the other hand you are saying alcohol is not causing you any problems. What are your thoughts on this?"*). When therapists use nonconfrontational back-to-back quizzical statements as shown in the above example, these statements are intended to help clients become aware of the contradictory or discrepant information in a way that minimizes defensiveness or resistance. Additionally, though young-adult problem drinkers may place high importance on doing well in their classes, getting a good job in the future, and being physically healthy, their frequent binge drinking and consequences serve to undermine their goals. For example, being hungover on school days or for family get-togethers may result in lower grades and angry parents. However, those dots can be hard to connect outside of the therapeutic setting, and that is where a motivational style can be helpful. Allowing clients to recognize their discrepancies and give voice to the change process is more likely to result in positive outcomes (Miller & Rollnick, 2012).

Rolling With Resistance

Resistance occurs when clients and therapists have two sets of values or goals in opposing directions. Therapists want clients to change, and often clients, particularly those coerced into treatment, do not see or feel they need to change. However, a motivational approach stresses that a reluctance to change is understandable and normal, particularly for many young-adult binge drinkers who do not see themselves as needing to change. It seems obvious that how a therapist responds to a client's resistance will affect the therapeutic relationship (Miller & Rollnick, 2012).

Resistance is often easy to recognize. When the clinical interaction does not feel right, it is a signal for therapists to use an MI approach that recognizes that therapists have a *choice* – increase resistance or roll with resistance. The more therapists challenge their clients, the more likely clients will become defensive. Such interactions are not productive and are referred to as a *righting reflex* (Miller & Rollnick, 2012); they occur when therapists attempt to set things right by telling clients what to do (e.g., *"If you don't stop drinking, you will end up in prison or dead"*).

An alternative to telling clients what to do is called *rolling with resistance*. Such an approach requires that a therapist acknowledge that a young-adult problem drinker is not ready to change or perhaps not even willing to discuss changing. When a therapist responds with reflections (*"What I hear you saying is that you are not ready to change and you do not even want to talk about your drinking right now"*), such reflections are more like to communicate to clients that their therapist understands them and is accepting of their autonomy.

Supporting Self-Efficacy

A major principle of MI is that it is a strengths-based approach, meaning it promotes the idea that clients have within themselves the tools and abilities to make positive changes. However, sometimes it is necessary for clinicians to help increase clients' senses of self-efficacy and their belief that they can be successful at making changes on their own. This is essentially working to improve clients' self-confidence, and can be accomplished by focusing on past successes rather than past failures, and highlighting the skills that clients have already been able to successfully implement, as a source of strength and hope for their future changes. Clinicians can help increase clients' feelings of self-efficacy by noting shifts in attitude or behavioral changes they have made so far. Specifically, it may be helpful to ask clients how they were able to accomplish a certain goal (e.g., *"When we met last time you were doubtful that you could go out without drinking at least eight drinks, but it looks like on Saturday you were able to stop with five. How were you able to do that?"* or *"You've said before that it was important to you not to drive after you've been drinking, and you seem to have been able to successfully avoid that over the last month. What do you think made that possible?"*). After clients have discussed how they were able to make certain changes, it is important for the therapist to ask how they feel about those changes. This often provides an opportunity for the clients to increase their self-confidence about their accomplishments. The importance of increasing clients' self-confidence is demonstrated by several studies that have shown that high levels of self-confidence at the end of treatment are associated with positive outcomes (Adamson, Sellman, & Frampton, 2009). (For a more in-depth discussion of broad MI strategies and techniques, such as asking permission, using open-ended questions, normalizing, and providing affirmations, see Mark and Linda Sobell's publicly available guide at http://www.nova.edu/gsc/forms/mi_rationale_techniques.pdf).

Readiness to Change

Another major tenet of MI is referred to as "meeting the client where they're at" in terms of behavior change. It is important to tailor the intervention to the client's level of motivation, which is a state and is thus dynamic and flexible. For example, if a therapist was meeting with a college student who was mandated to attend the session after an alcohol infraction on campus, and had already stated that he did not think there was anything wrong with his drinking, the therapist would meet the client where he's at if she were to ask him about the things he does and does not like about alcohol, in a nonjudgmental and eliciting manner (i.e., conduct a very low-level, exploratory intervention). However, if the clinician were to jump to asking him to make concrete goals about drink limits, that would likely be met with resistance because the intervention was farther ahead than his readiness to change level.

Assessing readiness to change is another very important part of MI, as readiness to change and motivation to change are very much connected. The idea of using clients' readiness to change as a starting place for MI is rooted in the stages of change model (discussed in detail in DiClemente, Schlundt, & Gemmell, 2004), which posits that clients are at one of five distinct stages of change when they begin treatment, and the goal of treatment is to move them along the continuum in the direction of change. Though it is possible to use this model to assess motivation at multiple points throughout treatment, this could be burdensome to client and therapist, and will likely not provide any incremental information beyond what could be obtained from using the readiness ruler (described in detail in the section "Readiness to Change"; see Section 3.6). The readiness ruler uses a scaling strategy (i.e., ratings of 1–10) with anchor points representing specific levels of readiness (e.g., *"I am definitely not ready to change," "I am thinking about making a change," "I am definitely ready to change"*). The use of this tool during the session is quick and easy to understand, and it allows clinicians to know immediately their clients' current motivational state (which, it should be noted, can change drastically week to week or even day to day). When a clinician is able to correctly identify a client's readiness to change, it is easier to map out intervention methods that are appropriate for where they are at and are thus more likely to be effective.

Clients who indicate that they are low in readiness to change are likely unaware of the risks or hazards that may be associated with their drinking. Should people find themselves in a mandatory treatment setting (i.e., participating in sessions they were mandated to attend), they may think it is because of bad luck or chance. High-risk college drinkers are often low in readiness to change, which is exhibited by engaging in potentially hazardous behaviors but not contemplating making any changes in those behaviors. When working with such clients, clinicians are advised to gently encourage them to consider the pros and cons of their drinking, while also presenting educational information about drinking norms, total hours and money spent, and specific feedback about the types of risks or hazards that they may have already experienced or are at risk of experiencing (i.e., conduct a personalized feedback intervention based on their individual assessments).

Clients who are slightly farther along on the Readiness Ruler may have begun to recognize the problems associated with their alcohol consumption and are perhaps thinking about change, but are not yet committed to making any specific changes. This can be thought of as ambivalence toward changing, with clients' levels of ambivalence being affected by many individual factors, including how much they have already thought about making a change, and whether or not family members or friends have ever had particularly dangerous or hazardous experiences with alcohol. Unlike many other problems of clinical concern (e.g., anxiety, depression), alcohol consumption is often positively associated with valued activities even when it is clearly creating problems for the drinker; thus, high ambivalence is quite understandable. Clinicians working with clients with this level of readiness should aim to help them resolve their ambivalence through increasing their belief that they will be successful in making the change. This can be done through a focus on improving their self-efficacy by pointing out areas of strength and determination already displayed or evidenced in other aspects of the client's life. Once clients indicate that they are ready and interested in making changes, clinicians can help them figure out the steps necessary to carry out those changes. Specifically, they can discuss different concrete goals (e.g., setting personal drink limits) or simply encourage clients to begin moving toward their goal (e.g., keeping track of the number of drinks consumed). Essentially, with clients who endorse this level of readiness, the clinician and client should work collaboratively to select the best change strategy to promote effectiveness. Additionally, it is important that the clinician provide ongoing praise, validation, and positivity as the client takes steps toward making healthy behavior changes. Some clients will report that they are quite far along in their readiness to change, perhaps even already exhibiting effort to modify or reduce their drinking and problematic behavior. Clients who have already started to make such changes are best helped when clinicians provide praise, support, and assistance with making change steps. This can take the form of self-efficacy promotion (*"So it looks like you were able to accomplish your goal of XYZ this week, how were you able to pull that off?"*), or even direct affirmation (*"The way you handled that situation demonstrates a lot of strength and commitment – it's impressive!"*). Additionally, for drinkers who have already started or succeeded in making changes, the goal of the clinician may shift to the prevention of relapse. In this case, the discussion would be focused on strategies to reduce vulnerability, both in terms of clients' general lifestyle as well as situations that are particularly high in temptation or risk.

Users of the readiness ruler within the MI framework highlight client resistance as an integral part of the intervention. Specifically, the presence of resistance is an indication that clinicians are ahead of their clients' level of readiness and should back up to meet them where they are, rather than combat the resistance or try to prove a point. Indeed, motivational techniques used within a harm-reduction framework embody a realistic view of heavy drinking and drinkers' reluctance to stop it, which is why proponents of these strategies view any progress toward change – even something as small as acknowledgment that some drinking practices may be dangerous – as a positive outcome of the intervention.

Mechanisms of Action in MI

Despite the difficulty inherent in isolating clear mechanisms of action of a communication style as opposed to a treatment, a great deal has been written about what potentially drives the success of an MI approach, and what clinicians should focus on when implementing it. MI-inconsistent behaviors on the part of the clinician (such as confronting, directing, and warning) have been found to be associated with poorer outcomes (Moyers & Martin, 2006), and these behaviors are less likely to be displayed by MI therapists than therapists affiliated with other modalities. As for client behaviors, those who receive MI are more likely to engage in *change talk* (Miller & Rollnick, 2012), which is associated with more positive substance use outcomes (Amrhein et al., 2003). Change talk involves clients themselves putting into words the needs, reasons, and benefits of making changes in their drinking behaviors. This is in comparison with other treatment styles in which therapists provide lectures or their own reasons for changing. Clinicians can elicit change talk from their clients by asking open-ended questions (*"What makes you think you need to change?"*) and allowing clients to respond based on what is most important to them personally. When changes in drinking behavior are slow to occur, change talk can take on more of an action-oriented direction (*"If you decided you wanted to change, what would you need to do to make that happen?"* [Note that this does not assume that clients are ready to change but allows them to voice what might happen if they were]).

Efficacy of Motivational Interviewing

Numerous research studies have shown that MI compared with a non-MI style can be characterized as an effective set of communication skills across a variety of health and mental health behaviors (Miller & Rollnick, 2012). A meta-analysis (Vasilaki, Hosier, & Cox, 2006) focusing on MIs delivered for problematic drinking that were delivered in a BI format found that a total of approximately 90 min of MI was more efficacious (in < 3-month follow-ups) than a no-treatment control in reducing alcohol consumption in a nondependent sample. Additionally, a total of approximately only 53 min of MI was more efficacious than an aggregated set of comparison treatments. As has been the case with efficacy studies of BIs, effect sizes of MI over comparison groups tend to decrease over time due to alternative treatment conditions catching up to MI, rather than MI clients returning to baseline.

Additionally, although very few studies have examined age as a predictor of outcome, some findings suggest that older clients are more responsive to MI (in terms of frequency of binge drinking) than younger clients (Shakeshaft, Bowman, Burrows, Doran, & Sanson-Fisher, 2002), although other studies using college student samples also reported favorable outcomes, so the role of age as a moderator of MI treatment outcome remains unclear.

4.3 Specific Implementation, Variation, and Combination of Methods

Many intervention programs consist of multiple components and are designed to reduce problem drinking through the use of several different therapeutic approaches. Some approaches will include feedback and behavior change advice; educational sessions about low-risk drinking, coping skills, and blood alcohol content; and interactive sessions aimed to modify alcohol expectancies and improve relaxation and general life balance. These types of multicomponent programs have been found to be effective for drinkers with varying degrees of risk, and one of the most widely used programs for young adults on college campuses is discussed in this section.

4.3.1 Brief Alcohol Screening and Intervention for College Students

One of the most empirically supported and widely used alcohol intervention programs on college campuses is BASICS (Dimeff et al., 1999). This program has been identified as a model program by the US Substance Abuse and Mental Health Services Administration (SAMHSA), and it has been associated with both preventive and harm-reduction outcomes. Though the delivery of the program can be flexible and modified based on client needs and therapist resources, the original BASICS intervention is conducted in an individual (not group) format over two 45–60-min sessions, with another 50 min of self-report questionnaire completion prior to or following the first session.

BASICS can be delivered to either light or heavy drinkers, though it was intended for young adults who already drink heavily and have experienced associated problems. When BASICS is delivered to heavy drinkers, it aims to ensure that existing problems do not get worse, as well as to prevent more serious problems from developing. That being said, BASICS is built on an intervention model aimed directly at college students who abuse alcohol and the particular characteristics of that drinking group. However, the developers invite practitioners working with different populations or in group settings to tailor the intervention as they see fit. Clinicians who deliver BASICS sessions or implement aspects of the treatment with their clients should be aware of the model's core assumptions: (a) many heavy drinkers lack the information and coping skills needed to drink moderately, (b) certain college and age-related milestones (such as living away from home) can contribute to heavy drinking, and (c) certain personal factors (such as having faulty beliefs about alcohol) and environmental factors (such as having particularly pressuring or heavy drinking friends) often work to inhibit drinkers' use of effective behavioral skills.

A brief review of the session content and components is provided below. Although clinicians do not need to undergo any formal training to deliver BASICS, a full tutorial is outside the scope of this book, and interested providers should consult the original treatment manual (Dimeff et al., 1999) for a full explanation of the session objectives, therapeutic style, and strategies to implement when working with a heavy drinking young-adult population.

The first session, referred to as the "Initial Assessment Interview," has two main objectives: (a) obtain information about the client's alcohol consumption and other health behaviors (this information is used in the second session), and (b) identify students for whom any alcohol consumption should be medically contraindicated (e.g., due to conditions like diabetes, ulcers, or a possible pregnancy). During this first session (and after building rapport with the students, orienting them to the structure and purpose of the sessions, and getting an initial commitment from the students to participate in the intervention), the BASICS protocol recommends that clinicians collect the following information:

Clients' typical quantity and frequency of alcohol consumption as well as atypical drinking occasions from the past 30 days (assessed through a daily drinking interview like the TLFB or other calendar-based assessment tool);

Clients' symptoms of AUD, conduct disorder, and other mental health problems (note that these are often assessed through brief checklist measures rather than interviews, and therefore may be given as part of the packet of self-report measures rather than during a session. Actual measures delivered vary by site and clinician);

Clients' family history of alcohol, substance use, or other mental health problems (often assessed using a family history measure, such as the Family Tree Questionnaire, described for use with young binge drinkers by Howland et al., 2010. Family history may also be best assessed through self-report measures prior to or following the interview session, which, like the symptom measures above, vary by site and clinician).

Once the assessment portion of the session is complete, clinicians provide clients with self-monitoring cards and requests that they record their drinking every day between the close of the initial meeting and the time of the next meeting (see the earlier section on self-monitoring within CBT for an explanation on the process and benefits of monitoring one's drinking; see the section "Self-Monitoring Techniques"). This marks the conclusion of the first session, and it is usually when students complete about 50 min of self-report questionnaires related to alcohol consumption, problems, and readiness to change (for a complete list of the self-administered measures, see the BASICS treatment manual: Dimeff et al., 1999).

The second session, referred to as the "Feedback Interview," takes place about 2 weeks after the initial session and primarily involves the provision of feedback and advice to students about their drinking, based on the information gathered during the assessment interview and from the self-report measures. The session begins with a review of students' self-monitoring cards, which serves to reestablish therapeutic rapport, as well as validate students for completing their assigned task. Clinicians can start by asking general questions like *"So what are your thoughts on filling out these cards every day?"* and *"After recording your drinking for two weeks, did you learn or notice anything about your drinking that you didn't know before?"* This should flow into a brief discussion of the monitoring process, and lead to more specific questions about students' drinking episodes (e.g., *"So let's take a look at how many drinks you usually drank on days you were drinking.... Were there any days on which you drank much more or much less than average?"*). With information about students' typical and peak consumption (as well as the time span of consumption and individual variables such as height and weight), therapists can provide clients with a personalized blood alcohol concentration (BAC) chart so they can estimate their own levels (see Appendix 5 for an example of a BAC chart). During this part of the session, therapists often include some psychoeducational information about alcohol use, such as the range of alcohol's effects, the meaning of tolerance and subjective intoxication, etc., but the developers caution clinicians to avoid lecturing or otherwise bombarding students with information, as this can end up creating distance between clinicians and students and serve to decrease overall engagement and motivation.

The remainder of the second session is spent reviewing students' personalized feedback reports, which are based on the information they provided in the first interview as well as the self-reported measures. Ideally, the feedback would be organized in a few pages with bullet points and corresponding graphics (as is often provided through computerized assessment printouts), but if therapists do not have access to such a format then whatever feedback format they use is likely sufficient (see the earlier section "Personalized Feedback" for publicly available assessment and feedback options). Though a much more detailed description of what to say and how to say it is provided in the manual (Dimeff et al., 1999), therapists should make sure to provide students with personalized feedback on the following topics: their present pattern of use as compared with peer norms of use, situational factors that contribute to heavy drinking, alcohol-related risks and consequences experienced (including emotional or behavioral consequences, family risk factors, and indices of the presence of an AUD), and general lifestyle and health behaviors. Throughout this second (and final) session, therapists are encouraged to give some advice and recommendations when it feels appropriate. This advice can be indirect, perhaps for the students to determine their own point of diminishing returns (when drinking more does not lead to having more fun), or it can be more direct, as when therapists specifically advise students with certain medical conditions to abstain from alcohol altogether and consult a physician. Most commonly, the advice deals with encouraging moderate instead of binge drinking, and providing students with specific strategies to do this.

Ideally, the session concludes with the therapist and student having some specific goals or plans in mind about how to apply BASICS to their lives, and this is best figured out by the students themselves after some open-ended prompting questions from the therapist, such as *"So what do you plan to do with all of the information we've covered?"* or *"How do you see yourself and your drinking changing as a result of this process?"* Students tend to be more open with their thoughts of change when approached in this manner rather than when they feel like they are being told they should or shouldn't do something in particular. Then, before leaving, students are given copies of their individualized feedback, plus a wallet-sized BAC card, tip sheet, and a list of local alcohol use resources.

The BASICS intervention incorporates almost all of the empirically supported treatment components discussed earlier; the general approach is harm reduction, the contents are based on CBT with personalized feedback, the format is brief, and it is delivered in a motivational style. Additionally, the techniques and approach of the original intervention described here can easily be expanded and adapted to other formats, such as small groups of college students, or even to nonstudents and individuals outside of college age. The BASICS manual describes the program as non-confrontational, non-judgmental, non-authoritarian, and non-labeling (Dimeff et al., 1999; all of which are consistent with the style of MI interactions), and a multitude of systematic research studies have found it to be effective in the reduction and prevention of heavy drinking.

Efficacy of BASICS

Studies comparing BASICS to assessment-only control conditions have found significant decreases in alcohol consumption and consequences both at a brief, 6-week follow-up assessment (Borsari & Carey, 2000) and over a 4-year period (Baer, Kivlahan, Blume, McKnight, & Marlatt, 2001). Additionally, a later study comparing BASICS to an educational intervention with a group discussion of college drinking and an assessment-only condition found that, at both 3- and 9-month follow-ups, heavier drinking participants who received the BASICS intervention showed larger reductions in weekly alcohol consumption and binge drinking frequency than heavier drinking participants in the other two conditions (Murphy et al., 2001). Those in the BASICS condition evaluated it more favorably than those in the education condition, suggesting it may be more popular and well received by both students and program developers than alternative intervention strategies across college campuses. Additional research has suggested that the efficacy of the BASICS intervention could be enhanced by combining it with a parent intervention (i.e., providing parents of incoming college students with a handbook with college drinking information and tips for having alcohol-related conversations with their children; Turrisi, Jaccard, Taki, Dunnam, & Grimes, 2001).

4.3.2 Other Intervention Avenues

Pharmacological Interventions

Pharmacological interventions are an empirically supported method of treating AUDs. However, their implementation is most common with severely dependent drinkers who have already gone through less "invasive" treatment options, and their efficacy is dependent on multiple factors, such as medication compliance, cost, and tolerance of potential side effects. Minimal research has been done on the use of medication to reduce alcohol consumption for people other than severely alcohol-dependent adults. Of the studies that have been conducted, many have methodological flaws such as small sample sizes, lack of condition blindness, or high dropout rates, which limit the strength of any seemingly positive findings. However, one recent randomized controlled trial (RCT) of young adults (18–25) conducted at an outpatient research center (O'Malley et al., in press) found that using Naltrexone – an opiate receptor blocking drug that has been approved by the US Food and Drug Administration (FDA) for treating alcohol dependence in adults – though not reducing frequency of drinking or number of heavy drinking days, did lead to decreased drinking intensity (i.e., number of drinks per drinking day and percentage of drinking days with an estimated BAC ≥ 0.08 g/dL). This is promising, given that some research has found that over 25% of college student drinkers would be receptive to a pharmacological intervention if they were going to "cut down or stop drinking" (Epler, Sher, Loomis, & O'Malley, 2009). Making pharmacotherapies available to young-adult drinkers makes particular clinical sense when thought about in the context of a stepped-care model, which proposes that the least intrusive and intense treatment option should be offered first, followed by more intensive courses of treatment (e.g., medication) if the initial course is unsuccessful. However, at the present time, pharmacotherapy for alcohol misuse has not yet been shown to be a first-line treatment for young problem drinkers and probably should not be considered unless multiple other interventions have failed. This picture may change, however, as more systematic, controlled research is conducted.

Brief Computer-Based and Mobile Programs

For adolescent and young-adult populations, computer, smartphone, and Internet-based intervention programs for alcohol misuse are steadily increasing in popularity because of their 24/7 accessibility and confidentiality. By 2015, more than 40% of the global population will have Internet access (International Telecommunication Union, 2014) which includes approximately 95% of those between the ages of 18 and 29 in the United States (Pew Research Center, 2014). Because young people use the Internet and their mobile devices so often and for so many purposes, having online alcohol resources "at their fingertips" may be an especially effective medium for engaging this population. Additionally, young adults often avoid or delay seeking in-person treatment for their problem drinking (because of a distrust of authority, fear they will be told to quit drinking completely, general ambivalence, or other reasons), making alternative and less personal treatment options more and more appealing. Currently, Internet programs concerning alcohol or drug problems exist in a variety of formats, including user-generated applications such as Web logs or blogs, Web-based instant messaging or discussion boards (e.g., http://AlcoholHelpCenter.net; Alcohol Help Center, 2013), as well as interactive alcohol feedback interventions and multisession programs (e.g., http://AlcoholEdu.com for mandated college students; EverFi, 2011), and smartphone apps (Mirtenbaum, Domingo, Fathi, Sobell, & Sobell, 2013). These Web-based and mobile sources offer self-assessments and screenings with catchy titles (e.g., "Find out if you're drinking too much!") as well as empirically supported cognitive behavioral intervention elements, such as

Attractive features of computer or Internet-based programs include anonymity, low or no cost, ease of accessibility, and instant provision of assessment results and feedback

formats for weighing one's own pros and cons of drinking (i.e., computerized decisional balance exercises), and suggestions for how to set individualized goals for reducing consumption and associated risks.

Online and mobile resources for alcohol misuse are appealing because they are unconstrained by geographic location and accessible 24 hr a day from the privacy and comfort of one's own home. They can be completed at the user's own pace, which allows individuals to utilize the tools when they are needed most. In addition, there is no risk of judgment from facilitators or peers, because the formats are anonymous, which may be especially appealing to adolescents and young adults who may be curious or minimally concerned about their drinking, but not worried enough to seek out a face-to-face intervention or resolved enough to commit to attend meetings or group sessions.

Efficacy of Brief Computer-Based and Mobile Programs

Although the research area is still relatively new, computer and Web-based interventions have been found to be efficacious in reducing drinking and alcohol-related consequences among young adults. In a randomized controlled pilot study of two different web-based methods designed for young-adult drinkers, researchers found that use of both an e-mail format and an iPhone app (iSelfChange™, a free evidence-based app for young adults to change their drinking, available at the iTunes store) led to a significant increase in the number of days abstinent and a significant decrease in alcohol-related consequences and percentage of binge drinking days in a national sample (Mirtenbaum et al., 2013). In another RCT, recipients of the commercially available program, the electronic Check-Up to GO (e-CHUG; http://www.e-chug.com) showed a significant decrease in their drinks per week and peak BAC compared with control participants at an 8-week follow-up. However, by the second follow-up at 16 weeks, the control groups had also reduced consumption to the point where there were no longer significant group differences (Walters, Vader, & Harris, 2007).

Because computer-delivered and web-based programs are efficacious, convenient, and inexpensive, and can easily be disseminated quickly and broadly, they are a natural choice for an early-stage intervention with problem drinkers. However, some evidence suggests that their effect is often short-term, and not as strong as in-person interventions. Thus, if resources are readily available and long-term change is a necessary goal, face-to-face alternatives are preferred.

4.4 Course of Young-Adult Alcohol Misuse

As was described in earlier sections, AUDs and heavy episodic binge drinking are more common among males, tend to peak in emerging adulthood (18–25), and decrease with age. In particular, heavy drinking has been found to decrease significantly during the mid-20s, a phenomenon referred to as maturing out. Indeed, most young people mature out of problem drinking without interventions. This has been attributed to the idea that late nights, hangovers, and potential alcohol-related consequences become incompatible with adult roles such as being a spouse, a parent, and a steady employee. Additionally, it has been found that personality changes commonly associated with adulthood (decreased impulsivity, decreased neuroticism) tend to accompany desistance in individuals who mature out of problematic drinking (Littlefield, Sher, & Wood, 2009). In contrast, the hazardous drinking and/or mild dependence that may seem common in young adults can progress into more severe alcohol dependence if people do not modify their drinking patterns as they take on more adult responsibilities. In severe cases in which people are having serious occupational, health, or relationship consequences as a result of their drinking and are not modifying their behavior in response, brief one-time interventions may be insufficient, and more intense and consistent outpatient treatment is likely required.

4.5 Emerging Treatments

Quite recently, several novel treatments have emerged as promising. These include cognitive bias modification (CBM), which aims to change individuals' maladaptive cognitive processes in relation to alcohol, as well as avenues targeting working memory, which work to increase drinkers' general control processes. The following emerging treatment approaches incorporate these strategies (as reviewed by Wiers, Gladwin, Hofmann, Salemink, & Ridderinkhof, 2013): (1) *attentional retraining* works to decrease drinkers' attentional biases toward alcohol-related cues, which can lead to increased motivation to change and reductions in drinking levels; (2) *evaluative conditioning and counterconditioning*, which is based on the finding that heavy drinkers have stronger positive and arousal associations with alcohol than light drinkers, works to challenge these biases by changing the nature of a drinkers' associations through repeated pairings of alcohol with negatively valenced pictures. Similarly, counterconditioning consists of a systematic pairing of an incentive cue (alcohol) with an aversive cue (e.g., a very bad tasting liquid). Both evaluative and counterconditioning approaches have demonstrated positive results in leading to changes in implicit alcohol associations; (3) *approach bias retraining* works to challenge problem drinkers' automatic tendencies to approach addiction-related stimuli, through modifying instructions in lab tasks (e.g., increasing the rate one should pull or push a lever, corresponding to approaching or avoiding a stimuli, respectively), and has been found to generate positive changes in approach biases among drinkers. Though more research needs to be conducted to further specify which cognitive biases are strongest, whether or not they can be addressed separately or simultaneously, and how these methods can be adapted to be used in common, nonlaboratory-intervention settings, initial findings of approaches targeting cognitive biases among problem drinkers appear to be encouraging.

However, implementing treatments to alter cognitive biases will be very difficult for many clinicians. For example, most therapists do not have access to joysticks and visual slides of beverages and valenced objects that would be needed to carry out some of these treatments as they are currently designed, and turn-key computer packages to deliver these interventions have yet to be developed and disseminated. This is acknowledged by the developers, who indicate that the next step is for CBM to be conducted through the use of widely available Internet programs, which would generate new possibilities for clinicians' arsenals of accessible treatment options. Therefore, although most clinicians might not be able to implement these emerging treatments as they currently are, treatment providers should remain on the lookout for more accessible formats of CBM, and those who are affiliated with research facilities already equipped with the necessary tools described above may find it interesting and effective to request access and begin utilizing them in a clinical fashion.

4.6 Problems Carrying Out Treatment

Though many of the treatment approaches that have been reviewed in this chapter have produced positive results, these interventions do not always go smoothly. Rather, working with young people on their alcohol misuse comes with a variety of potential problems. Although there is no exhaustive list of all the obstacles that could arise in the course of a given intervention strategy, this section highlights some common attitudes, behaviors, and outlooks that often and easily stand in the way of a positive treatment outcome.

4.6.1 Preintervention Obstacles

One common problem faced by clinicians working with young-adult drinkers involves the issue of referrals, or clients who are mandated to treatment. When young people are referred to an intervention, perhaps by their school, family, or physician, there is a good chance they are not happy about it. They may feel as though they are being unfairly labeled as an alcoholic, and that talking to a "professional" is an overreaction. In addition, depending on the reason for the referral, they may consider it unwarranted, or believe they are being unduly punished for something that was not their fault. Although these types of reactions will arise naturally (and are surely not limited to young people), the best way to approach such comments is likely with an emphasis on the broad, informal, and educational nature of the intervention. Often a reassuring statement about how people of all drinking levels have found X (insert specific activity) helpful will make clients feel less stigmatized, as will a reminder that no one will tell them they need to quit drinking. Most importantly, practitioners who are exposed to these types of concerns should listen to their clients and validate their feelings as understandable given the current situation. Even if clients do not immediately feel relieved, they will feel heard and know that the intervention is not designed to make them feel disordered or chastised.

4.6.2 In-Session Obstacles

When young adults are having difficulty with the feedback they receive in a session, a motivational approach will make them more receptive. Many individuals, particularly young adults, who are referred to an alcohol treatment program have reported being surprised to learn that their drinking is at a high or risky level (e.g., *"I don't normally drink like that!"* or *"My friends drink way more than I do"*). One of the reasons they are surprised to hear that their drinking is considered heavy or problematic is that young peoples' drinking most often does not parallel that of severely dependent drinkers or "chronic alcoholics" – they often do not drink every day, let alone throughout each day, nor have they experienced severe withdrawal effects or major life changes as a result of their drinking. (In our clinical experience, it is not uncommon for college student binge drinkers to answer with responses such as "homeless," "old," "sick," "unemployed," "drinks all day," or "has no family" when asked to describe someone with an alcohol problem.)

> **Clinical Pearl**
> **Refraining From Labels**
>
> When working with young-adult drinkers, clinicians should take particular care to refrain from labels (e.g., *"You are behaving like an alcoholic"*). Even suggestions of such sentiments increase client resistance and pullback.

Practitioners will have more success if they *roll with resistance* instead of labeling, accusing the client of being in denial or being confrontational (e.g., *"You wouldn't be here if you didn't have a problem"*). To best accomplish this, clinicians can reflect what the person says (e.g., *"It sounds like you are surprised to see that your average weekly drinking is in the top 20% of all drinkers"*). If a client says, *"I don't have any intention of quitting drinking,"* the clinician could respond with the following reflection: *"So it sounds like what you are saying is that abstinence is not something you feel comfortable with right now. I can understand that it is hard not to drink when many of your friends are partying. What do you think will happen if you get another arrest?"* Using reflections communicates that the clinician has heard and validated the client (though please note that validation and condoning a client's behavior are very different). Using such an approach will likely result in the client being more accepting and less resistant.

4.6.3 Postintervention Obstacles

Although clinicians may not be aware of how their clients are functioning after treatment ends, it is helpful to know what kinds of obstacles might interfere with the treatment plan. A common reason some problem drinkers do not change their behavior is because they have too few reasons for why they *should* change their behavior. When young people are only a few years into a drinking career, it is unlikely that they have experienced serious alcohol-related health or legal problems, nor any dire social or occupational consequences.

Further, for many young problem drinkers there are also a host of positive aspects or "good things" related to their drinking. Although there is no way to force anyone to change any behavior, discussions in treatment about things that might get in the way of them changing their drinking is a good relapse prevention technique. With the help of skilled clinicians, clients can be gently reminded of all the ways in which accomplishing certain moderate drinking goals may actually improve their social lives, as well as be encouraged to generate ways to prepare for inevitable setbacks.

The treatment methods described in this chapter, specifically harm-reduction approaches with motivational interviewing styles, have been found to be more effective in increasing motivation to change and compliance than more directive or instructional approaches that involve telling clients what to do. This is likely because young-adult problem drinkers – especially those who are mandated to treatment – are often skeptical of authority and rebel when they feel like they are being told what "not to do." Harm-reduction approaches and gentle, eliciting therapeutic styles create supportive and flexible environments, and thus lead to fewer displays of rebelliousness and better reception of clinicians' guidance.

4.7 Multicultural Issues

Documented differences in young-adult alcohol consumption and related problems suggest that, in general, White and Native American young adults drink more than African Americans and Asians, with consumption among Hispanics falling somewhere in the middle (NIAAA, 2006). Additionally, peak drinking ages differ across racial and ethnic groups, with Whites consuming the most between ages 19 and 22, and consumption among African Americans and Hispanics peaking later and lasting longer into adulthood.

These differences in levels and trends of consumption can influence the need for different treatment options and approaches for clients depending on their race, ethnicity, and cultural backgrounds. These variations can also be due to treatment need, access, appropriateness, and quality of care. Given equal amounts of alcohol consumption, ethnic minority populations experience more negative consequences as a result of drinking than Whites, making their need for treatment greater (e.g., Schmidt, Greenfield, & Mulia, 2006). However, research has continued to demonstrate that there are racial disparities in health care treatments, including treatments for alcohol misuse, that are above and beyond what is accounted for by differences in income and insurance coverage. Additionally, members of minority populations tend to have lower rates of treatment engagement, retention, and satisfaction with their care, though the reasons for all of these differences remain unclear. Indeed, a great deal more research on multicultural issues in treatment for young-adult alcohol misuse needs to be conducted to best determine the reasons and implications of treatment differences, as well as what clinicians can do about it with their own minority clients. It is important for clinicians to become as culturally sensitive and literate as possible when beginning treatment with clients from a minority population. This often includes receiving consultation from other clinicians, seeking out continuing education opportunities, and reading about cultural differences in alcohol consumption and specific techniques that have demonstrated effectiveness with the particular group. As is the case with nonminority clients, the goal is for the treatment to match or "fit" the cultural lifestyle, frame of mind, and experiences of the client. In order for minority clients to feel this "fit" and receive the most benefits from therapy, it may require clinicians to adapt more traditional or Anglo-oriented forms of treatment into treatments that are not necessarily geared toward mainstream, White, American young adults. (For more information on the role of culture in psychotherapy and what clinicians should do to be culturally competent, see Sue & Zane, 2009.)

4.8   Summary

What we have tried to communicate through this book is that using certain approaches and techniques when treating young-adult problem drinkers will make it easier to treat such individuals. Quite often, these drinkers are getting more "good things" out of their current drinking than "less good things," making the decision to cut back a difficult one. Further, because binge drinking is a relatively normative pattern among many young people on and off college campuses, it makes it difficult for them to recognize the existence of a problem.

We want to provide clinicians treating young problem drinkers with a toolkit of effective techniques, information, and strategies to help them motivate their clients to successfully change their alcohol use. In the "Description of Young-Adult Alcohol Misuse" chapter (see Chapter 1), we outlined some important aspects of young-adult drinking that clinicians should be aware of, such as drinking games, prepartying, and alcohol consequences, that are commonly experienced among this population. Additionally, we discussed diagnostic criteria for AUDs, which may not apply to all of the young binge drinkers who present for treatment but are important for clinicians to be familiar with when assessing the severity of a client's drinking problem. We also described common patterns of comorbidity with AUDs and the course of young-adult heavy drinking (specifically, the fact that many "mature out" of it at some point in their late 20s and 30s). In the chapter "Theories and Models of Alcohol Misuse" (see Chapter 2), we discussed the theories of pharmacological vulnerabilities, behavioral undercontrol, and affect regulation, and how certain individuals, such as those who have low sensitivity to alcohol or are high in impulsivity, may be at heightened risk for heavy consumption and alcohol-related problems according to these models. For clinicians, knowledge of these theories and what makes people more susceptible to drinking problems can be a helpful background and can provide some direction or areas of focus for treatment. In the third chapter, "Assessment and Treatment Indications" (see Chapter 3), we outlined the different types of assessments that may be useful for clinicians, from screening measures, to consequence measures, to diagnostic interviews and the readiness ruler. These assessments not only help inform clinicians of clients' starting points at the outset of treatment, but continued use of them during sessions can help to monitor progress and guide the course of treatment in the direction of change. Often assessment feedback alone is sufficient to motivate people to change. In this last chapter, "Treatment" (see Chapter 4), we discussed in some detail the harm-reduction approach, specific aspects of CBT and PFIs, BIs and stepped care, and why a MI style and approach can be used to motivate clients to change or consider changing their drinking, even when they are not ready for, or are ambivalent about, changing. A hallmark of all behavioral and cognitive interventions is an individualized treatment approach. That is, we recognize that each client will present with different concerns and problems and as such will require a unique combination of empirically supported treatments. There is no one-size-fits-all program or standard treatment for all young-adult problem drinkers. Instead we suggest that those reading this book use it as a guide for developing their own assessment and interventions with young problem drinkers.

5

Further Reading

Correia, C. J., Murphy, J. G., & Barnett, N. P. (2012). *College student alcohol abuse: A guide to assessment, intervention, and prevention*. New York, NY: Wiley.
  This book contains multiple contributions from well-respected researchers in the fields of alcohol misuse and problem drinking among college students. Chapter subjects range from a discussion of the prevalence and consequences of alcohol misuse, to a review of clinical assessment tools, to the implementation of stepped care in the college setting.

National Institute on Alcohol Abuse and Alcoholism. (2007). *Rethinking drinking: Alcohol and your health* (NIG23 publication No. 09-3770). Washington, DC: US Government Printing Office.
  This interactive website, sponsored by the National Institute on Alcohol Abuse and Alcoholism, includes an extensive amount of information and resources for people interested in cutting back on their drinking or simply learning more about alcohol use in general. Visitors to the website are able to get feedback on their drinking patterns and level of risk, read tips for reducing their drinking, and complete and/or print out worksheets (e.g., to weigh the pros and cons of drinking, to keep track of daily drinks). This website is also a good resource for clinicians who are looking for free, easily accessible information and tools that can be used with heavy drinking clients.

National Research Council and Institute of Medicine. (2004). *Reducing underage drinking: A collective responsibility.* Washington, DC: The National Academies Press.
  This book, published by the National Research Council (which is organized by the National Academy of Sciences), provides a review of the characteristics and consequences of underage drinking as well as a picture of the public approach to this behavior – including media-driven encouragement as well as community-based policies and interventions aimed to discourage underage drinking.

Baer, J. S., Dimeff, L. A., Marlatt, G. A., & Kivlahan, D. R. (1999). *Brief Alcohol Screening and Intervention for College Students (BASICS): A harm reduction approach.* New York, NY: The Guilford Press.
  This instructive manual for the BASICS course walks the reader through the common patterns of problematic drinking seen among college students, the theoretical bases of the intervention (harm reduction and motivational interviewing), and a step-by-step guide for how the course is implemented. It also provides a thoughtful discussion of clinical considerations and the types of obstacles that facilitators may face when delivering the intervention.

Vander Ven, T. (2011). *Getting wasted: Why college students drink too much and party so hard.* New York, NY: New York University Press.
  This easy-to-read book describes the heavy drinking lifestyle common among college students, and explains the destructive behaviors in terms of social needs and support, rather than an individual drive for excess.

6

References

Abbey, A. (2002). Alcohol-related sexual assault: A common problem among college students. *Journal of Studies on Alcohol and Drugs, Suppl. 14*, 118–128.

Adamson, S. J., Sellman, J. D., & Frampton, C. M. A. (2009). Patient predictors of alcohol treatment outcome: A systematic review. *Journal of Substance Abuse Treatment, 36*(1), 75–86. http://doi.org/10.1016/j.jsat.2008.05.007

Agrawal, S., Sobell, M. B., & Sobell, L. C. (2008). The Timeline Followback: A scientifically and clinically useful tool for assessing substance use. In R. F. Belli, F. P. Stafford, & D. F. Alwin (Eds.), *Calendar and time diary methods in life course research* (pp. 57–68). Beverly Hills, CA: Sage.

American Psychiatric Association. (1994). *Diagnostic and statistical manual of mental disorders* (4th ed.). Washington, DC: Author.

American Psychiatric Association. (2013). *Diagnostic and statistical manual of mental disorders* (5th ed.) Washington, DC: Author.

Amrhein, P. C., Miller, W. R., Yahne, C. E., Palmer, M., & Fulcher, L. (2003). Client commitment language during motivational interviewing predicts drug use outcomes. *Journal of Consulting and Clinical Psychology, 71*(5), 862–878. http://doi.org/10.1037/0022-006X.71.5.862

APA Practice Organization – Practice Central. (2014). *ICD-10 implementation delayed until October 2015*. Retrieved from http://www.apapracticecentral.org/update/2014/04-10/icd-10-delayed.aspx

Baer, J. S., Kivlahan, D. R., Blume, A. W., McKnight, P., & Marlatt, G. A. (2001). Brief intervention for heavy drinking college students: Four-year follow-up and natural history. *American Journal of Public Health, 98*, 1310–1316. http://doi.org/10.2105/AJPH.91.8.1310

Baker, T., Piper, M., McCarthy, D., Majeskie, M., & Fiore, M. (2004). Addiction motivation reformulated: An affective processing model of negative reinforcement. *Psychological Review, 111*(1), 33–51. http://doi.org/10.1037/0033-295X.111.1.33

Bandura, A. (2006). Toward a psychology of human agency. *Perspectives on Psychological Science, 1*(2), 164–180. http://doi.org/10.1111/j.1745-6916.2006.00011.x

Babor, T. F., Higgins-Biddle, J. C., Saunders, J. B., & Monteiro, M. G. (2001). *AUDIT: The Alcohol Use Disorders Identification Test: Guidelines for use in primary care.* (2nd ed.). Geneva, Switzerland: World Health Organization.

Barnett, N. P., Orchowski, L. M., Read, J. P., & Kahler, C. W. (2013). Predictors and consequences of pregaming using day-and week-level measurements. *Psychology of Addictive Behaviors, 27*(4), 921–933. http://doi.org/10.1037/a0031402

Barry, A. E. (2007). Using theory-based constructs to explore the impact of Greek membership on alcohol-related beliefs and behaviors: A systematic literature review. *Journal of American College Health, 56*(3), 307–315. http://doi.org/10.3200/JACH.56.3.307-316

Barry, A. E., Stellefson, M. L, Piazza-Gardner, A. K., Chaney, B. H., & Dodd, V. (2013). The impact of pregaming on subsequent blood alcohol concentrations: An event-level analysis. *Addictive Behaviors, 38*(8), 2374–2377. http://doi.org/10.1016/j.addbeh.2013.03.014

Bechara, A. (2005). Decision making, impulse control and loss of willpower to resist drugs: A neurocognitive perspective. *Nature Neuroscience, 8,* 1458–1463. http://doi.org/10.1038/nn1584

Bertholet, N., Daeppen, J. B., Wietlisbach, V., Fleming, M., & Burnand, B. (2005). Reduction of alcohol consumption by brief alcohol intervention in primary care: systematic review and meta-analysis. *Archives of Internal Medicine, 165*(9), 986–995. http://doi.org/10.1001/archinte.165.9.986

Blomqvist, J. (2002). Recovery with and without treatment: A comparison of resolutions of alcohol and drug problems. *Addiction Research & Theory, 10*(2), 119–158. http://doi.org/10.1080/16066350290017248

Booth, P. G., Dale, B., Slade, P. D., & Dewey, M. E. (1992). A follow-up study of problem drinkers offered a goal choice option. *Journal of Studies on Alcohol and Drugs, 53*(6), 594–600.

Borsari, B., Bergen-Cico, D., & Carey, K. B. (2003). Self-reported drinking-game participation of incoming college students. *Journal of American College Health, 51*(4), 149–154. http://doi.org/10.1080/07448480309596343

Borsari, B., & Carey, K. B. (2000). Effects of a brief motivational intervention with college student drinkers. *Journal of Consulting and Clinical Psychology, 68*(4), 728–733. http://doi.org/10.1037/0022-006X.68.4.728

Breslin, F. C., Sobell, L. C., Sobell, M. B., & Agrawal, S. (2000). A comparison of a brief and long version of the Situational Confidence Questionnaire. *Behaviour Research and Therapy, 38*(12), 1211–1220. http://doi.org/10.1016/S0005-7967(99)00152-7

Carey, K. B., Carey, M. P., Henson, J. M., Maisto, S. A., & DeMartini, K. S. (2011). Brief alcohol interventions for mandated college students: comparison of face-to-face counseling and computer-delivered interventions. *Addiction, 106*(3), 528–537.

Carey, K. B., Scott-Sheldon, L. A., Carey, M. P., & DeMartini, K. S. (2007). Individual-level interventions to reduce college student drinking: A meta-analytic review. *Addictive behaviors, 32*(11), 2469–2494. http://doi.org/10.1016/j.addbeh.2007.05.004

Cederbaum, A. I. (2012). Alcohol metabolism. *Clinics in Liver Disease, 16*, 667–685. http://doi.org/10.1016/j.cld.2012.08.002

Chung, T., & Martin, C. S. (2005). What were they thinking?: Adolescents' interpretations of DSM-IV alcohol dependence symptom queries and implications for diagnostic validity. *Drug and Alcohol Dependence, 80*(2), 191–200. http://doi.org/10.1016/j.drugalcdep.2005.03.023

Connors, G. J., & Maisto, S. A. (2003). Drinking reports from collateral individuals. *Addiction, 98*(2), 21–29. http://doi.org/10.1046/j.1359-6357.2003.00585.x

Conrod, P. J., O'Leary-Barrett, M., Newton, N., Topper, L., Castellanos-Ryan, N., Mackie, C., & Girard, A. (2013). Effectiveness of a selective, personality-targeted prevention program for adolescent alcohol use and misuse: a cluster randomized controlled trial. *Journal of American Medical Association Psychiatry, 70*(3), 334–42.

Cooper, M. (1994). Motivations for alcohol use among adolescents: Development and validation of a four-factor model. *Psychological Assessment, 6*(2), 117–128. http://doi.org/10.1037/1040-3590.6.2.117

Cyders, M. A., Smith, G. T., Spillane, N. S., Fischer, S., Annus, A. M., & Peterson, C. (2007). Integration of impulsivity and positive mood to predict risky behavior: Development and validation of a measure of positive urgency. *Psychological Assessment, 19*(1), 107–118. http://doi.org/10.1037/1040-3590.19.1.107

Dawson, D. A., Goldstein, R. B., & Grant, B. F. (2013). Differences in the profiles of DSM-IV and DSM-5 alcohol use disorders: Implications for clinicians. *Alcoholism: Clinical and Experimental Research, 37*(s1), E305–E313.

Dawson, D. A., Grant, B. F., & Li, T. K. (2005). Quantifying the risks associated with exceeding recommended drinking limits. *Alcoholism: Clinical and Experimental Research, 29*, 902–908. http://doi.org/10.1097/01.ALC.0000164544.45746.A7

DeGue, S. (2014). *Preventing sexual violence on college campuses: Lessons from research and practice* (Prepared for the White House Task Force to Protect Students from Sexual Assault). Retrieved from https://www.notalone.gov/assets/evidence-based-strategies-for-the-prevention-of-sv-perpetration.pdf

Dick, D. M, Smith, G., Olausson, P., Mitchell, S. H., Leeman, R. F, O'Malley, S. S., & Sher, K. (2010). Understanding the construct of impulsivity and its relationship to alcohol use disorders. *Addiction Biology, 15*(2), 217–226. http://doi.org/10.1111/j.1369-1600.2009.00190.x

DiClemente, C. C., Schlundt, D., & Gemmell, L. (2004). Readiness and stages of change in addiction treatment. *American Journal on Addictions, 13*(2), 103–119. http://doi.org/10.1080/10550490490435777

Dimeff, L. A., Baer, J. S., Kivlahan, D. R., & Marlatt, G. A. (1999). *Brief alcohol screening and intervention for college students*. London: Guilford Press.

Donovan, J. E. (1993). Young adult drinking-driving: Behavioral and psychosocial correlates. *Journal of Studies on Alcohol and Drugs, 54*(5), 600–613.

Edwards, G., & Gross, M. M. (1976). Alcohol dependence: provisional description of a clinical syndrome. *British Medical Journal, 1*(6017), 1058–1061.

Edwards, A. C., & Kendler, K. S. (2012). Twin study of the relationship between adolescent attention-deficit/hyperactivity disorder and adult alcohol dependence. *Journal of Studies on Alcohol and Drugs, 73*(2), 185–194.

Edwards, G. (1986). The Alcohol Dependence Syndrome: A concept as stimulus to enquiry. *British Journal of Addiction, 81*(2), 171–183. http://doi.org/10.1111/j.1360-0443.1986.tb00313.x

Epler, A. J., Sher, K. J., Loomis, T. B., & O'Malley, S. S. (2009). College student receptiveness to various alcohol treatment options. *Journal of American College Health, 58*(1), 26–32. http://doi.org/10.3200/JACH.58.1.26-32

EverFi. (2011, November). *Outside the classroom: AlcoholEdu for college students*. Retrieved from https://alcoholedu.com/

Alcohol Help Center. (2013). *Welcome to Alcohol Help Center 2.0* [Website]. Evolution Health Systems, Inc. Retrieved from http://www.alcoholhelpcenter.net/.

Farrell, M., Howes, S., Bebbington, P., Brugha, T., Jenkins, R., Lewis, G., . . . Meltzer, H. (2001). Nicotine, alcohol and drug dependence and psychiatric comorbidity Results of a national household survey. *The British Journal of Psychiatry, 179*(5), 432–437. http://doi.org/10.1192/bjp.179.5.432

First, M. B., Williams, J. B., Karg, R. S., & Spitzer, R. L. (2014). *Structured Clinical Interview for DSM-5 Disorders – Research Version (SCID-5-RV)*. Arlington, VA: American Psychiatric Association.

Fromme, K., Stroot, E. A., & Kaplan, D. (1993). Comprehensive effects of alcohol: Development and psychometric assessment of a new expectancy questionnaire. *Psychological Assessment, 5*(1), 19–26. http://doi.org/10.1037/1040-3590.5.1.19

Giancola, P. R. (2000). Executive functioning: a conceptual framework for alcohol-related aggression. *Experimental and Clinical Psychopharmacology, 8*(4), 576–597. http://doi.org/10.1037/1064-1297.8.4.576

Grant, B. F., Dawson, D. A., Stinson, F. S., Chou, P. S., Dufour, M. C., & Pickering, R. (2004). The 12-month prevalence and trends in DSM-IV alcohol abuse and dependence: United States, 1991–1992 and 2001–2002. *Drug and Alcohol Dependence, 74*, 223–234. http://doi.org/10.1016/j.drugalcdep.2004.02.004

Grant, V. V., Stewart, S. H., O'Connor, R. M., Blackwell, E., & Conrod, P. J. (2007). Psychometric evaluation of the five-factor Modified Drinking Motives Questionnaire: Revised in undergraduates. *Addictive Behaviors, 32*(11), 2611–2632. http://doi.org/10.1016/j.addbeh.2007.07.004

Ham, L. S., Stewart, S. H., Norton, P., & Hope, D. A. (2005). Psychometric assessment of the Comprehensive Effects of Alcohol Questionnaire: Comparing a brief version to the original full scale. *Journal of Psychopathology and Behavioral Assessment, 27*, 141–158. http://doi.org/10.1007/s10862-005-0631-9

Heather, N., Smailes, D., & Cassidy, P. (2008). Development of a readiness ruler for use with alcohol brief interventions. *Drug and Alcohol Dependence, 98*(3), 235–240. http://doi.org/10.1016/j.drugalcdep.2008.06.005

Howland, J., Rohsenow, D. J., Greece, J. A., Littlefield, C. A., Almeida, A., Heeren, T., . . . Hermos, J. (2010). The effects of binge drinking on college students' next-day academic test-taking performance and mood state. *Addiction, 105*(4), 655–665. http://doi.org/10.1111/j.1360-0443.2009.02880.x

International Telecommunication Union. (2014). *The world in 2009: ICT facts and figures*. Retrieved from http://www.itu.int/en/ITU-D/Statistics/Pages/stat/default.aspx

Jones, B. T. (2004). Changing alcohol expectancies: Techniques for altering motivations for drinking. In W. M. Cox & E. Klinger (Eds.), *Handbook of motivational counseling* (pp. 373–387). Chichester, UK: John Wiley & Sons, Ltd.

Jones, B. T., Corbin, W., & Fromme, K. (2001). A review of expectancy theory and alcohol consumption. *Addiction, 96*(1), 57–72. http://doi.org/10.1046/j.1360-0443.2001.961575.x

Kahler, C. W., Strong, D. R., & Read, J. P. (2005). Toward efficient and comprehensive measurement of the alcohol problems continuum in college students: The brief young adult alcohol consequences questionnaire. *Alcoholism: Clinical and Experimental Research, 29*, 1180–1189. http://doi.org/10.1097/01.ALC.0000171940.95813.A5

Kahler, C. W., Strong, D. R., Read, J. P., Palfai, T. P., & Wood, M. D. (2004). Mapping the continuum of alcohol problems in college students: a Rasch model analysis. *Psychology of Addictive Behaviors, 18*(4), 322–333. http://doi.org/10.1037/0893-164X.18.4.322

Kessler, R. C., Chiu, W. T., Demler, O., & Walters, E. E. (2005). Prevalence, severity, and comorbidity in the national comorbidity survey replication. *Archives of General Psychiatry, 62*, 617–627. http://doi.org/10.1001/archpsyc.62.6.617

Kessler, R. C., Crum, R. M., Warner, L. A., Nelson, C. B., Schulenberg, J., & Anthony, J. C. (1997). Lifetime co-occurrence of DSM-III-R alcohol abuse and dependence with other psychiatric disorders in the National Comorbidity Survey. *Archives of General Psychiatry, 54*(4), 313–321. http://doi.org/10.1001/archpsyc.1997.01830160031005

Kessler, R. C., & Üstün, T. B. (2004). The World Mental Health (WMH) Survey Initiative version of the World Health Organization (WHO) Composite International Diagnostic Interview (CIDI). *International Journal of Methods in Psychiatric Research, 13*(2), 93–121. http://doi.org/10.1002/mpr.169

Klingemann, H. K., & Sobell, L. C. (2007). *Promoting self-change from addictive behaviors: Practical implications for policy, prevention, and treatment*. New York, NY: Springer. http://doi.org/10.1007/978-0-387-71287-1

Krueger, R. F., Helzer, J. E., & Hudziak, J. J. (2002). Psychometric perspectives on comorbidity. In J. E. Helzer & J. J. Hudziak (Eds.), *Defining psychopathology in the 21st century: DSM–V and beyond* (pp. 41–54). Washington, D.C.: American Psychiatric Publishing, Inc.

Kuther, T. L. (2002). Rational decision perspectives on alcohol consumption by youth: Revising the theory of planned behavior. *Addictive Behaviors, 27*, 35–47. http://doi.org/10.1016/S0306-4603(00)00161-1

LaBrie, J., Ehret, P., & Hummer, J. (2013). Are they all the same? An exploratory, categorical analysis of drinking game types. *Addictive Behaviors, 38*, 2133–2139. http://doi.org/10.1016/j.addbeh.2012.12.002

Larimer, M. E., & Cronce, J. M. (2007). Identification, prevention, and treatment revisited: Individual-focused college drinking prevention strategies 1999–2006. *Addictive Behaviors, 32*, 2439–2468. http://doi.org/10.1016/j.addbeh.2007.05.006

Lee, C. M., Lewis, M. A., & Neighbors, C. (2009). Preliminary examination of spring break alcohol use and related consequences. *Addictive Behaviors, 23*(4), 689–694. http://doi.org/10.1037/a0016482

Littlefield, A. K., Sher, K. J., & Wood, P. K. (2009). Is "maturing out" of alcohol involvement related to personality change? *Journal of Abnormal Psychology, 118*, 360–374. http://doi.org/10.1037/a0015125

Littlefield, A., Vergés, A., Rosinski, J., Steinley, D., & Sher, K. (2013). Motivational typologies of drinkers: do enhancement and coping drinkers form two distinct groups? *Addiction, 108*(3), 497–503. http://doi.org/10.1111/j.1360-0443.2012.04090.x

Malloy, E. A., Goldman, M., & Kington, R. (2002). *A call to action: Changing the culture of drinking at U.S. colleges*. Washington, DC: National Institute on Alcohol Abuse and Alcoholism, Task Force of the National Advisory Council on Alcohol Abuse and Alcoholism.

Marlatt, G. A., & Donovan, D. D. M. (2005). Relapse prevention for alcohol and drug problems. In G. A. Marlatt & D. M. Donovan (Eds.), *Relapse prevention: Maintenance strategies in the treatment of addictive behaviors* (pp. 1–42). New York: Guilford Press.

Marlatt, G. A., & Witkiewitz, K. (2002). Harm reduction approaches to alcohol use: Health promotion, prevention, and treatment. *Addictive Behaviors, 27*, 867–886. http://doi.org/10.1016/S0306-4603(02)00294-0

Martin, C. S., Sher, K. J., & Chung, T. (2011). Hazardous use should not be a diagnostic criterion for substance use disorders in DSM-5. *Journal of Studies on Alcohol and Drugs, 72,* 685–686.

Martin, C. S., Steinley, D. L., Vergés, A., & Sher, K. J. (2011). The proposed 2/11 symptom algorithm for DSM-5 substance-use disorders is too lenient. *Psychological Medicine, 41,* 2008–2014. http://doi.org/10.1017/S0033291711000717

Martinez, J. A., Steinley, D. A., & Sher, K. J. (2010). Deliberate induction of alcohol tolerance: Empirical introduction to a novel health risk. *Addiction, 105,* 1767–1770. http://doi.org/10.1111/j.1360-0443.2010.03042.x

McBride, N., Midford, R., Farringdon, F., & Phillips, M. (2000). Early results from a school alcohol harm minimization study: the School Health and Alcohol Harm Reduction Project. *Addiction, 95*(7), 1021–1042. http://doi.org/10.1046/j.1360-0443.2000.95710215.x

Miller, W. R., & Rollnick, S. (2012). *Motivational interviewing: Helping people change* (3rd ed.). New York, NY: Guilford Press.

Mirtenbaum, D. E., Domingo, S., Fathi, D. F., Sobell, L. C., Sobell, M. B., Rubizovsky, T., . . . Bronsburg, S. E. (2013, November). *Randomized controlled trial of an evidence-based alcohol intervention using two social media formats: iPhone and email.* Poster presented at the 47th annual meeting of the Association for Behavioral and Cognitive Therapies, Nashville, TN (ABCT Addictive Behaviors SIG Outstanding Student Poster Award).

Morgenstern, J., & Longabaugh, R. (2000). Cognitive-behavioral treatment for alcohol dependence: a review of evidence for its hypothesized mechanisms of action. *Addiction, 95*(10), 1475–1490. http://doi.org/10.1046/j.1360-0443.2000.951014753.x

Moyer, A., Finney, J. W., Swearingen, C. E., & Vergun, P. (2002). Brief interventions for alcohol problems: a meta-analytic review of controlled investigations in treatment-seeking and non-treatment-seeking populations. *Addiction, 97,* 279–292. http://doi.org/10.1046/j.1360-0443.2002.00018.x

Moyers, T. B., & Martin, T. (2006). Therapist influence on client language during motivational interviewing sessions. *Journal of Substance Abuse Treatment, 30*(3), 245–251. http://doi.org/10.1016/j.jsat.2005.12.003

Moyers, T. B., & Miller, W. R. (2013). Is low therapist empathy toxic? *Psychology of Addictive Behaviors, 27*(3), 878–884. http://doi.org/10.1037/a0030274

Murphy, J. G., Correia, C. J., Colby, S. M., & Vuchinich, R. E. (2005). Using behavioral theories of choice to predict drinking outcomes following a brief intervention. *Experimental and Clinical Psychopharmacology, 13*(2), 93–101. http://doi.org/10.1037/1064-1297.13.2.93

Murphy, J. G., Duchnick, J. J., Vuchinich, R. E., Davison, J. W., Karg, R. S., Olson, A. M., . . . Coffey, T. T. (2001). Relative efficacy of a brief motivational intervention for college student drinkers. *Psychology of Addictive Behaviors, 15*(4), 373–379. http://doi.org/10.1037/0893-164X.15.4.373

National Institute on Alcohol Abuse and Alcoholism. (2006). *Alcohol alert: Young adult drinking* (Number 68). Retrieved from http://pubs.niaaa.nih.gov/publications/aa68/aa68.htm

National Institute on Alcohol Abuse and Alcoholism. (2007a). *Alcohol alert: Alcohol and tobacco* (Number 71). Retrieved from http://pubs.niaaa.nih.gov/publications/AA71/AA71.pdf

National Institute on Alcohol Abuse and Alcoholism. (2007b). *Rethinking drinking: Alcohol and your health* (NIH Publication No. 09–3770). Washington, DC: US Government Printing Office. Retrieved from http://rethinkingdrinking.niaaa.nih.gov/default.asp

National Institute of Alcohol Abuse and Alcoholism. (2011). *Five year strategic plan: Alcohol.* Washington, DC: Author. Retrieved from http://pubs.niaaa.nih.gov/publications/StrategicPlan/NIAAASTRATEGICPLAN.htm

National Institute on Alcohol Abuse and Alcoholism. (2014). *Drinking levels defined.* Retrieved from http://www.niaaa.nih.gov/alcohol-health/overviewalcohol-consumption/moderate-binge-drinking

National Registry of Evidence-based Programs and Practices. (2014). *Challenging college alcohol abuse.* Retrieved from http://www.nrepp.samhsa.gov/ViewIntervention.aspx?id=60

Neal, D. J., Corbin, W. R., & Fromme, K. (2006). Measurement of alcohol-related consequences among high school and college students: application of item response models to the Rutgers Alcohol Problem Index. *Psychological Assessment, 18*(4), 402–414. http://doi.org/10.1037/1040-3590.18.4.402

Neighbors, C., Atkins, D. C., Lewis, M. A., Lee, C. M., Kaysen, D., Mittmann, A., …. Rodriguez, L.M. (2011). Event-specific drinking among college students. *Psychology of Addictive Behaviors, 25*(4), 702–707. http://doi.org/10.1037/a0024051

Neighbors, C., Lee, C. M., Atkins, D. C., Lewis, M. A., Kaysen, D., Mittman, A., … Larimer, M. E. (2012). A randomized controlled trial of event-specific prevention strategies for reducing problematic drinking associated with 21st birthday celebrations. *Journal of Consulting and Clinical Psychology, 80*(5), 850–862. http://doi.org/10.1037/a0029480

Nelson, R. O., & Hayes, S. C. (1981). Theoretical explanations for reactivity in self-monitoring. *Behavior Modification, 5*, 3–14. http://doi.org/10.1177/014544558151001

O'Malley, P. M. (2004). Maturing out of problematic alcohol use. *Alcohol Research and Health, 28*(4), 202–204.

O'Malley, S. O., Corbin, W. R., Leeman, R. F., DeMartini, K. S., Fucito, L. M., Ikomi, J., … Kranzler, H. R. (in press). Naltrexone reduces drinking in young adults: A double-blind, randomized clinical trial of efficacy and safety. *Journal of Clinical Psychiatry.*

O'Neill, S. E., Parra, G. R., & Sher, K. J. (2001). Clinical relevance of heavy drinking during the college years: Cross-sectional and prospective perspectives. *Psychology of Addictive Behaviors, 15*(4), 350–359. http://doi.org/10.1037/0893-164X.15.4.350

Pew Research Center. (2014). *Teens fact sheet.* Retrieved from http://www.pewinternet.org/fact-sheets/teens-fact-sheet/

Quinn, P. D., & Fromme, K. (2011). Subjective response to alcohol challenge: A quantitative review. *Alcoholism: Clinical and Experimental Research, 35*(10), 1759–70. http://doi.org/10.1111/j.1530-0277.2011.01521.x

Read, J. P., Kahler, C. W., & Strong, D. R. (2006). Development and preliminary validation of the Young Adult Alcohol Consequences Questionnaire. *Journal of Studies on Alcohol, 67,* 169–177.

Rehm, J., Mathers, C., Popova, S., Thavorncharoensap, M., Teerawattananon, Y., & Patra, J. (2009). Global burden of disease and injury and economic cost attributable to alcohol use and alcohol-use disorders. *The Lancet, 373*(9682), 2223–2233. http://doi.org/10.1016/S0140-6736(09)60746-7

Reinert, D. F., & Allen, J. P. (2007). The alcohol use disorders identification test: An update of research findings. *Alcoholism: Clinical and Experimental Research, 31*(2), 185–199. http://doi.org/10.1111/j.1530-0277.2006.00295.x

Rendón-Ramírez, A., Cortés-Couto, M., Martínez-Rizo, A. B., Muñiz-Hernández, S., & Velázquez-Fernández, J. B. (2013). Oxidative damage in young alcohol drinkers: A preliminary study. *Alcohol, 47*(7), 501–504. http://doi.org/10.1016/j.alcohol.2013.08.002

Roberts, B. W., Walton, K., & Viechtbauer, W. (2006). Patterns of mean-level change in personality traits across the life course: A meta-analysis of longitudinal studies. *Psychological Bulletin, 132,* 1–25. http://doi.org/10.1037/0033-2909.132.1.1

Roy, M., Dum, M., Sobell, L. C., Sobell, M. B., Simco, E. R., Manor, H., & Palmerio, R. (2008). Comparison of the Quick Drinking Screen and the Alcohol Timeline Followback with outpatient alcohol abusers. *Substance Use & Misuse, 43*(14), 2116–2123. http://doi.org/10.1080/10826080802347586

Rutledge, P. C., Park, A., & Sher, K. J. (2008). 21st birthday drinking: extremely extreme. *Journal of Consulting and Clinical Psychology, 76*(3), 511–516. http://doi.org/10.1037/0022-006X.76.3.511

Saladin, M. E., & Santa Ana, E. J. (2004). Controlled drinking: more than just a controversy. *Current Opinion in Psychiatry, 17*(3), 175–187. http://doi.org/10.1097/00001504-200405000-00005

Schmidt, L., Greenfield, T., & Mulia, N. (2006). Unequal treatment: racial and ethnic disparities in alcoholism treatment services. *Alcohol Research and Health, 29*(1), 49.

Schuckit, M. A., Smith, T. L., & Tipp, J. E. (1997). The Self-Rating of the Effects of Alcohol (SRE) form as a retrospective measure of the risk for alcoholism. *Addiction, 92,* 979–988. http://doi.org/10.1111/j.1360-0443.1997.tb02977.x

Shakeshaft, A. P., Bowman, J. A., Burrows, S., Doran, C. M., & Sanson-Fisher, R. W. (2002). Community-based alcohol counseling: a randomized clinical trial. *Addiction, 97*(11), 1449–1463. http://doi.org/10.1046/j.1360-0443.2002.00199.x

Sher, K. J., & Trull, T. J. (1996). Methodological issues in psychopathology research. *Annual Review of Psychology, 47,* 371–400. http://doi.org/10.1146/annurev.psych.47.1.371

Sobell, M. B., & Sobell, L. C. (2000). Stepped care as a heuristic approach to the treatment of alcohol problems. *Journal of Consulting and Clinical Psychology, 68*(4), 573–579. http://doi.org/10.1037/0022-006X.68.4.573

Sobell, L. C., & Sobell, M. B. (2008). *Motivational interviewing strategies and techniques: Rationales and examples.* Retrieved from http://www.nova.edu/gsc/forms/mi_rationale_techniques.pdf

Sobell, L. C., & Sobell, M. B. (2011). *Group therapy with substance abuse disorders: A motivational cognitive-behavioral approach.* New York, NY: Guilford Press.

Stinson, F. S., Grant, B. F., Dawson, D. A., Ruan, W. J., Huang, B., & Saha, T. (2005). Comorbidity between DSM-IV alcohol and specific drug use disorders in the United States: Results from the National Epidemiologic Survey on Alcohol and Related Conditions. *Drug and Alcohol Dependence, 80,* 105–116. http://doi.org/10.1016/j.drugalcdep.2005.03.009

Sue, S., & Zane, N. (2009, August). *The role of culture and cultural techniques in psychotherapy: A critique and reformulation.* Paper presented at the Asian American Psychological Association convention, Los Angeles, CA, US, August, 1985.

Torgersen, S., Kringlen, E., & Cramer, V. (2001). The prevalence of personality disorders in a community sample. *Archives of General Psychiatry, 58*(6), 590–596. http://doi.org/10.1001/archpsyc.58.6.590

Tragesser, S. L., Sher, K. J., Trull, T. J., & Park, A. (2007). Personality disorder symptoms, drinking motives, and alcohol use and consequences: Cross-sectional and prospective mediation. *Experimental and Clinical Psychopharmacology, 15,* 282–292. http://doi.org/10.1037/1064-1297.15.3.282

Turrisi, R., Jaccard, J., Taki, R., Dunnam, H., & Grimes, J. (2001). Examination of the short-term efficacy of a parent intervention to reduce college student drinking tendencies. *Psychology of Addictive Behaviors, 15,* 366–372. http://doi.org/10.1037/0893-164X.15.4.366

US Departments of Agriculture and of Health and Human Services. (2010). *Dietary guidelines for Americans.* Washington, DC: Author.

Vakili, S., Sobell, L. C., Sobell, M. B., Simco, E. R., & Agrawal, S. (2008). Using the Timeline Followback to determine time windows representative of annual alcohol consumption with problem drinkers. *Addictive Behaviors, 33*(9), 1123–1130. http://doi.org/10.1016/j.addbeh.2008.03.009

Vasilaki, E. I., Hosier, S. G., & Cox, W. M. (2006). The efficacy of motivational interviewing as a brief intervention for excessive drinking: A meta-analytic review. *Alcohol & Alcoholism, 41*(3), 328–335. http://doi.org/10.1093/alcalc/agl016

Vergés, A., Haeny, A. M., Jackson, K. M., Bucholz, K. K., Grant, J. D., Trull, T. J., . . . Sher, K. J. (2013). Refining the notion of maturing out: Results from the National Epidemiologic Survey on Alcohol and Related Conditions. *American Journal of Public Health, 103,* e67–e73. http://doi.org/10.2105/AJPH.2013.301358

Vergés, A., Jackson, K. M., Bucholz, K. K., Grant, J. D., Trull, T. J., Wood, P. K., & Sher, K. J. (2012). Deconstructing the age-prevalence curve of alcohol dependence: Why 'maturing out' is only a small piece of the puzzle. *Journal of Abnormal Psychology, 121*(2), 511–523. http://doi.org/10.1037/a0026027

Walters, S. T., & Neighbors, C. (2005). Feedback interventions for college alcohol misuse: What, why and for whom? *Addictive Behaviors, 30*(6), 1168–1182. http://doi.org/10.1016/j.addbeh.2004.12.005

Walters, S. T., Vader, A. M., & Harris, T. R. (2007). A controlled trial of Web-based feedback for heavy drinking college students. *Prevention Science, 8*(1), 83–88. http://doi.org/10.1007/s11121-006-0059-9

Wechsler, H. (1996). Fraternities, sororities and binge drinking: Results from a national study of American colleges. *NASPA Journal, 33*(4), 260–279.

Wechsler, H., Lee, J. E., Kuo, M., & Lee, H. (2000). College binge drinking in the 1990s: A continuing problem results of the Harvard School of Public Health 1999 College Alcohol Study. *Journal of American College Health, 48*(5), 199–210. http://doi.org/10.1080/07448480009599305

Wechsler, H., & Nelson, T. F. (2001). Binge drinking and the American college students: What's five drinks? *Psychology of Addictive Behaviors, 15*(4), 287–291. http://doi.org/10.1037/0893-164X.15.4.287

White, H. R., Young Mun, E., Pugh, L., & Morgan, T. J. (2007). Long-term effects of brief substance use interventions for mandated college students: Sleeper effects of an in-person personal feedback intervention. *Alcoholism: Clinical and Experimental Research, 31*(8), 1380–1391. http://doi.org/10.1111/j.1530-0277.2007.00435.x

White, W. L. (2000). Addiction as a disease: Birth of a concept. *Addiction, 51*, 73.

Wiers, R. W., Gladwin, T. E., Hofmann, W., Salemink, E., & Ridderinkhof, K. R. (2013). Cognitive bias modification and cognitive control training in addiction and related psychopathology mechanisms, clinical perspectives, and ways forward. *Clinical Psychological Science, 1*(2), 192–212. http://doi.org/10.1177/2167702612466547

Witkiewitz, K., & Marlatt, G. A. (2004). Relapse prevention for alcohol and drug problems: That was Zen, this is Tao. *American Psychologist, 59*(4), 224–235 http://doi.org/10.1037/0003-066X.59.4.224

Wood, P. K., Sher, K. J., & Rutledge, P. C. (2007). College student alcohol consumption, day of the week, and class schedule. *Alcoholism: Clinical and Experimental Research, 31*(7), 1195–1207. http://doi.org/10.1111/j.1530-0277.2007.00402.x

World Health Organization. (2008). *ICD-10: International statistical classification of diseases and related health problems* (10th rev. ed.). New York, NY: Author.

World Health Organization. (2014). *ICD-11 beta draft*. Retrieved from http://apps.who.int/classifications/icd11/browse/f/en

7

Appendix: Tools and Resources

Appendix 1: The Alcohol Use Disorders Identification Test: Self-Report Version
Appendix 2: Daily Drinking Log
Appendix 3: Example of a Personalized Feedback Profile
Appendix 4: Questions That Evoke Change Talk
Appendix 5: Effects at Specific Blood Alcohol Concentration (BAC) Levels

The Alcohol Use Disorders Identification Test: Self-Report Version

Instructions: Because alcohol use can affect your health and can interfere with certain medications and treatments, it is important that we ask some questions about your use of alcohol. Your answers will remain confidential so please be honest.

Place an X in one box that best described your answers to each question.

Questions	0	1	2	3	4	
1. How often do you have a drink containing alcohol?	Never	Monthly or less	2–4 times a month	2–3 times a week	4 or more times a week	
2. How many drinks containing alcohol do you have on a typical day when you are drinking?	1 or 2	3 or 4	5 or 6	7 to 9	10 or more	
3. How often do you have five or more drinks on one occasion?	Never	Less than Monthly	Monthly	Weekly	Daily/ Almost daily	
4. How often during the last year have you found that you were not able to stop drinking once you had started?	Never	Less than Monthly	Monthly	Weekly	Daily/ Almost daily	
5. How often during the last year have you failed to do what was normally expected of you because of drinking?	Never	Less than Monthly	Monthly	Weekly	Daily/ Almost daily	
6. How often during the last year have you needed a drink first thing in the morning?	Never	Less than Monthly	Monthly	Weekly	Daily/ Almost daily	
7. How often during the last year have you had a feeling of guilt or remorse after drinking?	Never	Less than Monthly	Monthly	Weekly	Daily/ Almost daily	
8. How often during the last year have you been unable to remember what happened the night before because of your drinking?	Never	Less than Monthly	Monthly	Weekly	Daily/ Almost daily	
9. Have you or someone else been injured because of your drinking?	Never	Less than Monthly	Monthly	Weekly	Daily/ Almost daily	
10. Has a relative, friend, doctor, or other health care worker been concerned about your drinking or suggested you cut down?	Never	Less than Monthly	Monthly	Weekly	Daily/ Almost daily	
	TOTAL					

Notes. Scoring: Items are scored on a scale of 0–4, allowing for a total possible score of 40. Those who score at or above an 8 are typically considered to be hazardous or problem drinkers. Adapted from Babor, Higgins-Biddle, Saunders, & Monteiro, (2001).

This page may be reproduced by the purchaser for personal/professional use.
From: R. P. Winograd & K. J. Sher: *Binge Drinking and Alcohol Misuse Among College Students and Young Adults*

© 2015 Hogrefe Publishing

Daily Drinking Log

Day/Date	Total # of drinks	Any high-risk factors present?	What feelings and thoughts were associated with your drinking?	Did your drinking cause you problems?
	If you didn't drink, write "0"	Y = Yes, N = No If "Y" please specify	(e.g., excitement, stress, boredom)	Y = Yes, N = No If "Y" please specify
Monday / /				
Tuesday / /				
Wednesday / /				
Thursday / /				
Friday / /				
Saturday / /				
Sunday / /				

Weekly Total # of Drinks =

This page may be reproduced by the purchaser for personal/professional use.
From: R. P. Winograd & K. J. Sher: *Binge Drinking and Alcohol Misuse Among College Students and Young Adults*

© 2015 Hogrefe Publishing

Example of a Personalized Feedback Profile

Where Does Your Drinking Fit In?
The average number of drinks you reported consuming per week was 16 drinks. How do you compare with American women of your age? You can use the following graph to see how much you drink as compared with American women 18 to 29 years old. The striped segment is where your drinking falls on the chart.

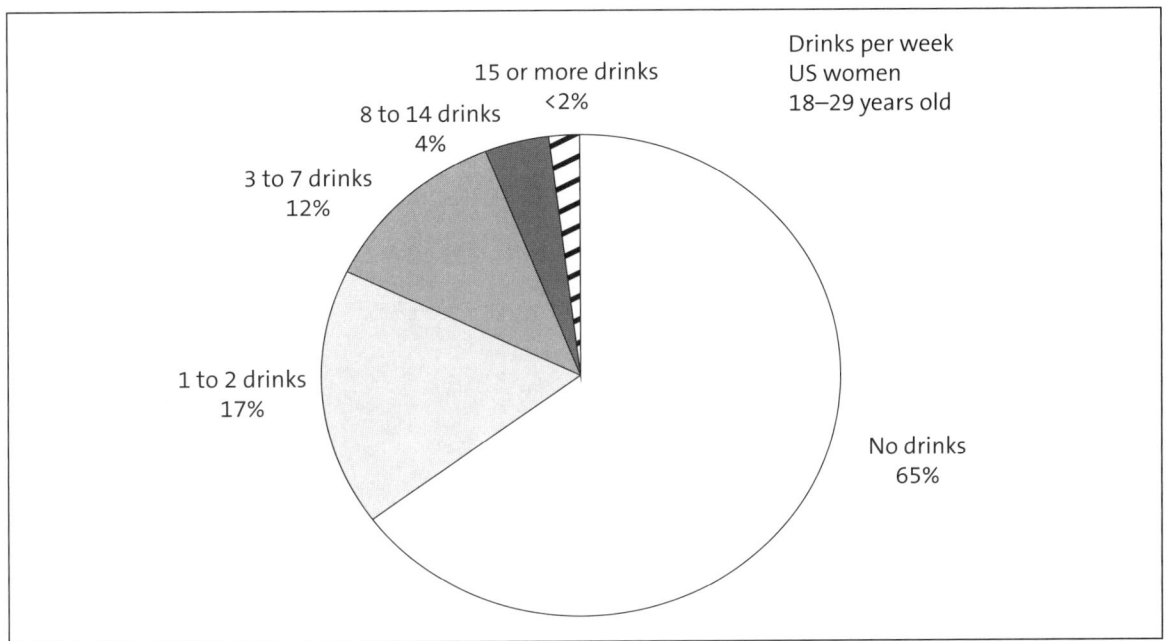

What About Me?

Based on your typical drinking during one week:
- You reported drinking on 43% of all the days last year.
- You also reported that you drank a total of 832 drinks in the last year.

This means that:
- You spent from $1,248 to $3,328 in the last year, depending on where you drank (e.g., at home, in a bar).
- You also consumed, on average, 500 added calories per drinking day from alcohol.

Risky Drinking
A national survey conducted in 1994 looked at how much people drink in a week and how their drinking might be affecting different areas of their lives. People were asked about their physical health, outlook on life, friends/social life, relationships with spouse/partner and children, home life, financial position and work or studies. Not surprisingly, the results showed that the more people drank in a week, the greater the chance that the drinking was affecting more and more areas of their lives.

How likely are you to have problems as a result of your drinking? The striped bar on the chart below shows where you fit.

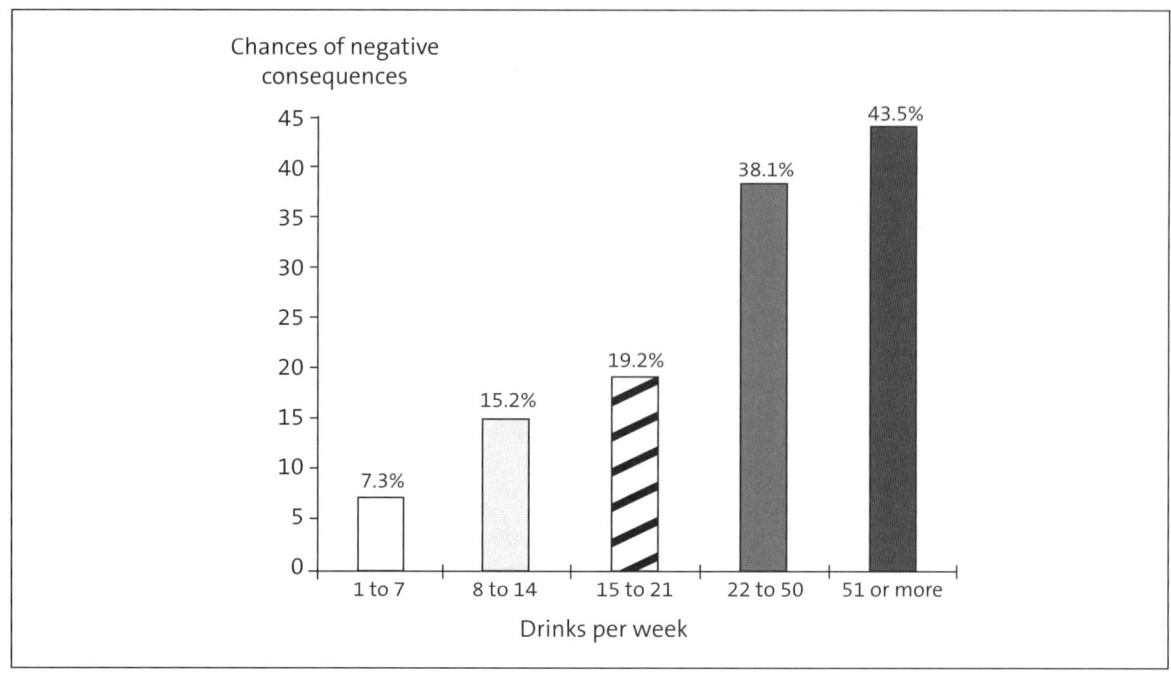

Heavy Drinking Days
Drinking more than five drinks on one occasion is heavy drinking. This type of drinking places you at increased risk of experiencing negative consequences because of your drinking. If you got rid of these heavy drinking days, you would reduce your chance of experiencing problems by about 50%.

Alcohol-Related Consequences
In fact, you experienced some consequences related to your drinking. The X shows which of the following alcohol-related problems you reported experiencing in the last year. When people stop or reduce heavy drinking these consequences will often decrease or disappear.

In the last year, your drinking had a harmful effect on…

	your friendships or social life
	your physical health
	your outlook on life (happiness)
	your home life or marriage
X	your work, studies, or employment opportunities
X	your financial position

See http://notes.camh.net/efeed.nsf/feedback for a personalized alcohol use feedback form.

Questions That Evoke Change Talk

Disadvantage of Status Quo

Problem Recognition
- What makes you think that you may need to make a change?
- What things make you think that your drinking is a problem?
- What difficulties have you had in relation to your drinking?
- In what ways do you think you or other people have been harmed by your drinking?
- In what ways has this been a problem for you?
- What makes you feel like you shouldn't keep on drinking the way you have been?

Concern
- What is there about your drinking that you or other people might see as reasons for concern?
- What worries you about your drinking?
- What can you imagine happening to you as a result of your drinking?
- How do you feel about your drinking? How much does that concern you?
- In what ways does this concern you?
- What do you think will happen if you don't make a change?

Advantages of Change
- How would you like things to be different?
- What would be some good things about quitting drinking?
- What would you like your life to be like in 5 years?
- If you could make this change immediately, by magic, how would things be different?
- What would be the advantages of making this change?

Optimism About Change
- What makes you think that if you decide to make a change in your drinking that you could do it?
- What encourages you to feel like you can change if you want to?
- What do you think would work for you, if you decided to change?
- What would make you feel even more confident that you could make a change?
- When else in your life have you made a big change like this? How did you do it?
- What personal strengths do you have that will help you succeed?

Intention to Change
- If you could easily make any changes with your drinking, what would be different?
- Where are you in terms of your smoking at this point?
- I can see that you're feeling stuck at the moment. What's going to have to change?
- Never mind the "how" for right now, what do you want to have happen?
- How important is this to you? How much do you want to do this?
- What would you be willing to try?
- What do you intend to do?

Compiled by BASICS project staff at the University of Missouri–Columbia, MO, USA. Reprinted with permission. This page may be reproduced by the purchaser for personal/professional use.

From: Winograd, R. P., & Sher, K. J. (2015). *Binge drinking and alcohol misuse among college students and young adults.* Boston, MA: Hogrefe Publishing.

Effects at Specific Blood Alcohol Concentration (BAC) Levels

The effects of alcohol intoxication are greatly influenced by individual variations among users. Some users may become intoxicated at a much lower blood alcohol concentration (BAC) level than is shown.

BAC, g/dL	Effects
0.02–0.03	No loss of coordination, slight euphoria and loss of shyness. Depressant effects are not apparent. Mildly relaxed and maybe a little lightheaded.
0.04–0.06	Feeling of well-being, relaxation, lower inhibitions, sensation of warmth. Euphoria. Some minor impairment of reasoning and memory, lowering of caution. Your behavior may become exaggerated and emotions intensified (Good emotions are better, bad emotions are worse).
0.07–0.09	Slight impairment of balance, speech, vision, reaction time, and hearing. Euphoria. Judgment and self-control are reduced, and caution, reason and memory are impaired, 0.08 is legally impaired and it is illegal to drive at this level. You will probably believe that you are functioning better than you really are.
0.10–0.125	Significant impairment of motor coordination and loss of good judgment. Speech may be slurred; balance, vision, reaction time and hearing will be impaired. Euphoria.
0.13–0.15	Gross motor impairment and lack of physical control. Blurred vision and major loss of balance. Euphoria is reduced and dysphoria (anxiety, restlessness) is beginning to appear. Judgment and perception are severely impaired.
0.16–0.19	Dysphoria predominates, nausea may appear. The drinker has the appearance of a "sloppy drunk."
0.20	Felling dazed, confused or otherwise disoriented. May need help to stand or walk. If you injure yourself you may not feel the pain. Some people experience nausea and vomiting at this level. The gag reflex is impaired and you can choke if you do vomit. Blackouts are likely at this level so you may not remember what has happened.
0.25	All mental, physical and sensory functions are severely impaired. Increased risk of asphyxiation from choking on vomit and of seriously injuring yourself by falls or other accidents.
0.30	STUPOR. You have little comprehension of where you are. You may pass out suddenly and be difficult to awaken.
0.35	Coma is possible. This is the level of surgical anesthesia.
0.40 and up	Onset of coma, and possible death due to respiratory arrest.

Reprinted with permission. B.R.A.D. (1999). *Effects at specific B.A.C. levels*. Retrieved from http://www.brad21.org/effects_at_specific_bac.html, © 1999 by B.R.A.D.
This page may be reproduced by the purchaser for personal/professional use.
From: Winograd, R. P., & Sher, K. J. (2015). *Binge drinking and alcohol misuse among college students and young adults*. Boston, MA: Hogrefe Publishing.

Stephen A. Maisto, Gerard J. Connors, Ronda L. Dearing

Alcohol Use Disorders

Advances in Psychotherapy – Evidence-Based Practice, Vol. 10

2007, viii+ 94 pages,
ISBN 978-0-88937-317-4
US $29.80 / £ 19.90 / € 24.95

Practice-oriented, evidence-based guidance on treating alcohol problems – one of the most widespread health problems in modern society.

This volume in the series *Advances in Psychotherapy – Evidence-Based Practice* provides therapists and students with practical and evidence-based guidance on the diagnosis and treatment of alcohol problems.

Alcohol abuse and alcohol dependence are widespread, and the individual and societal problems associated with these disorders have made the study and treatment of alcohol use disorders a clinical research priority. Research over the past several decades has led to the development of excellent empirically supported treatment methods. This book aims to increase clinicians' access to empirically supported interventions for alcohol use disorders, with the hope that these methods will become the standard in clinical practice.

Table of Contents
1. **Description of Alcohol Use Disorders:** Terminology • Definition • Epidemiology • Course and Prognosis • Differential Diagnosis • Comorbidities • Diagnostic Procedures and Documentation
2. **Theories and Models of Alcohol Use Disorders:** Traditional Theories of AUDs • Biopsychosocial Model of AUDs
3. **Diagnosis and Treatment Indications:** Introduction • General Guidelines and Considerations • Drinking History • Life-Functioning • Prioritizing Problems and Needs • Referral Issues
4. **Treatment:** Introduction and Overview • Behavioral and Psychological Methods • Brief Interventions (BIs) • Extensions of Basic CBT • Psychopharmacological Methods • Mutual (Peer) Self-Help Groups • Efficacy and Prognosis • Combination of Treatment Methods • Problems in Carrying Out Treatment • Multicultural Considerations
5. **Further Reading**
6. **References**
7. **Appendix: Tools and Resources**

"As a teacher of graduate courses on substance abuse, I have long waited for a book like this. An excellent review of evidence-based assessment and treatment methods, presented at an easily understood yet high level, objectively, and with valuable clinical advice."
Mark B. Sobell, PhD

"This book provides a remarkably clear, comprehensive, but succinct, coverage of our current understanding of how best to help people with alcohol use disorders. Everything the practicing clinician needs to know is there."
Nick Heather, PhD

Hogrefe Publishing
30 Amberwood Parkway · Ashland, OH 44805 · USA
Tel: (800) 228-3749 · Fax: (419) 281-6883
E-Mail: customerservice@hogrefe.com

Hogrefe Publishing
Merkelstr. 3 · 37085 Göttingen · Germany
Tel: +49 551 999 500 · Fax: +49 551 999 50 111
E-Mail: customerservice@hogrefe.de

Hogrefe Publishing c/o Marston Book Services Ltd
160 Eastern Ave., Milton Park · Abingdon, OX14 4SB · UK
Tel: +44 1235 465577 · Fax +44 1235 465556
direct.orders@marston.co.uk

Order online at **www.hogrefe.com**
or call toll-free **(800) 228-3749** (US only)

View all volumes at www.hogrefe.com/series/apt

Vol. 1: **Bipolar Disorder** by R. P. Reiser, L. W. Thompson, ISBN 978-0-88937-310-5
Vol. 2: **Heart Disease** by J. A. Skala, K. E. Freedland, R. M. Carney, ISBN 978-0-88937-313-6
Vol. 3: **Obsessive-Compulsive Disorder** by J. S. Abramowitz, ISBN 978-0-88937-316-7
Vol. 4: **Childhood Maltreatment** by C. Wekerle, A. L. Miller, D. A. Wolfe, C. B. Spindel, ISBN 978-0-88937-314-3
Vol. 5: **Schizophrenia** by S. M. Silverstein, W. D. Spaulding, A. A. Menditto, ISBN 978-0-88937-315-0
Vol. 6: **Treating Victims of Mass Disaster and Terrorism** by J. Housley, L. E. Beutler, ISBN 978-0-88937-321-1
Vol. 7: **Attention-Deficit/Hyperactivity Disorder in Children and Adults** by A. U. Rickel, R. T. Brown, ISBN 978-0-88937-322-8
Vol. 8: **Problem and Pathological Gambling** by J. P. Whelan, T. A. Steenbergh, A. W. Meyers, ISBN 978-0-88937-312-9
Vol. 9: **Chronic Illness in Children and Adolescents** by R. T. Brown, B. P. Daly, A. U. Rickel, ISBN 978-0-88937-319-8
Vol. 10: **Alcohol Use Disorders** by S. A. Maisto, G. J. Connors, R. L. Dearing, ISBN 978-0-88937-317-4
Vol. 11: **Chronic Pain** by B. J. Field, R. A. Swarm, ISBN 978-0-88937-320-4
Vol. 12: **Social Anxiety Disorder** by M. M. Antony, K. Rowa, ISBN 978-0-88937-311-2
Vol. 13: **Eating Disorders** by S. W. Touyz, J. Polivy, P. Hay, ISBN 978-0-88937-318-1
Vol. 14: **Suicidal Behavior** by R. McKeon, ISBN 978-0-88937-327-3
Vol. 15: **Substance Use Problems** by M. Earleywine, ISBN 978-0-88937-329-7
Vol. 16: **Elimination Disorders in Children and Adolescents** by E. R. Christophersen, P. C. Friman, ISBN 978-0-88937-334-1
Vol. 17: **Sexual Violence** by W. R. Holcomb, ISBN 978-0-88937-333-4
Vol. 18: **Depression** by L. P. Rehm, ISBN 978-0-88937-326-6
Vol. 19: **Hypochondriasis and Health Anxiety** by J. S. Abramowitz, A. E. Braddock, ISBN 978-0-88937-325-9
Vol. 20: **Public Health Tools for Practicing Psychologists** by J. A. Tucker, D. M. Grimley, ISBN 978-0-88937-330-3
Vol. 21: **Nicotine and Tobacco Dependence** by A. L. Peterson, M. W. Vander Weg, C. R. Jaén, ISBN 978-0-88937-324-2
Vol. 22: **Nonsuicidal Self-Injury** by E. D. Klonsky, J. J. Muehlenkamp, S. P. Lewis, B. Walsh, ISBN 978-0-88937-337-2
Vol. 23: **Growing Up with Domestic Violence** by P. G. Jaffe, D. A. Wolfe, M. Campbell, ISBN 978-0-88937-336-5
Vol. 24: **Generalized Anxiety Disorder** by Craig Marker, Alyson Aylward, ISBN 978-0-88937-335-8
Vol. 25: **Sexual Dysfunction in Women** by Marta Meana, ISBN 978-0-88937-400-3

Also available as E-books. Search for
- "Hogrefe Advances" at **amazon.com/kindle**
- "Hogrefe Advances" at **bn.com/nook**
- "Hogrefe Publishing" in the iBookstore/iTunes

Hogrefe Publishing
30 Amberwood Parkway · Ashland, OH 44805 · USA
Tel: (800) 228-3749 · Fax: (419) 281-6883
E-Mail: customerservice@hogrefe.com

Hogrefe Publishing
Merkelstr. 3 · 37085 Göttingen · Germany
Tel: +49 551 999 500 · Fax: +49 551 999 50 111
E-Mail: customerservice@hogrefe.de

Hogrefe Publishing c/o Marston Book Services Ltd
160 Eastern Ave., Milton Park· Abingdon, OX14 4SB · UK
Tel: +44 1235 465577 · Fax +44 1235 465556
direct.orders@marston.co.uk

Order online at **www.hogrefe.com**
or call toll-free **(800) 228-3749** (US only)

Alan L. Peterson, Mark W. Vander Weg & Carlos Roberto Jaén

Nicotine and Tobacco Dependence

Advances in Psychotherapy – Evidence-Based Practice, Vol. 21

2011, x + 94 pages
US $29.80 / £ 19.90 / € 24.95
ISBN 978-0-88937-324-2

How to stop patients and clients smoking – guidance on treatments that work, from leading US authorities.

This volume in the series *Advances in Psychotherapy: Evidence-Based Practice* provides health care providers with practical and evidence-based guidance on the diagnosis and treatment of nicotine and tobacco dependence. Tobacco use is the leading preventable cause of death in the world, and it is the only legally available consumer product that kills people when used entirely as intended. Research over the past several decades has led to the development of a number of evidence-based treatments for nicotine and tobacco dependence that can be delivered by health care professionals in a variety of primary and specialty care settings. This book aims to increase medical, mental health, and dental practitioners' access to empirically supported interventions for nicotine and tobacco dependence, with the hope that these methods will be incorporated into routine clinical practice.

The book is both a compact "how-to" reference for clinicians and an ideal educational resource for students and for practice-oriented continuing education. The volume includes tables, boxed clinical pearls, and clinical vignettes, and the appendix includes clinical tools, patient handouts, and links to the top recommended websites for the download of additional patient materials.

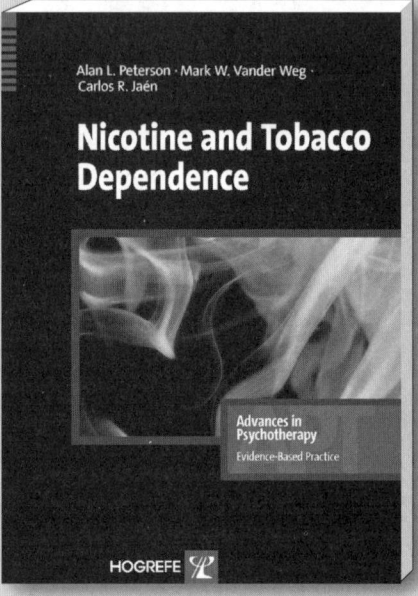

For further details visit
www.hogrefe.com

Hogrefe Publishing
30 Amberwood Parkway · Ashland, OH 44805 · USA
Tel: (800) 228-3749 · Fax: (419) 281-6883
E-Mail: customerservice@hogrefe.com

Hogrefe Publishing
Merkelstr. 3 · 37085 Göttingen · Germany
Tel: +49 551 999 500 · Fax: +49 551 999 50 111
E-Mail: customerservice@hogrefe.de

Hogrefe Publishing c/o Marston Book Services Ltd
160 Eastern Ave., Milton Park· Abingdon, OX14 4SB · UK
Tel: +44 1235 465577 · Fax +44 1235 465556
direct.orders@marston.co.uk

Order online at **www.hogrefe.com**
or call toll-free **(800) 228-3749** (US only)